Building an Entrepreneurial Organisation

Entrepreneurship is often focused on understanding new ventures, but the entrepreneurial flame is required in growing organisations too. This textbook examines how organisations can become more entrepreneurial to achieve sustainable growth.

The authors show how entrepreneurship can be used to address crisis points of growth within small firms and to overcome the limitations of stagnation within large firms. By integrating entrepreneurship and innovation management, the book presents a framework to diagnose entrepreneurial behaviour within existing firms. Drawing upon research and reflecting practice across a range of industries, from football, through Silicon Valley, to the retail sector, it includes insights from leading practitioners.

The authors build an understanding of entrepreneurship in context to provide diagnostic tools to help organisations make entrepreneurship central to their culture. This unique text is therefore useful reading for business students from advanced undergraduate to executive education.

Simon Mosey is a Professor and Director of the Haydn Green Institute for Innovation and Entrepreneurship at the University of Nottingham. He is editor of the *Journal of Technology Transfer,* and his research interests address technology entrepreneurship, entrepreneurship education and innovation management. He is co-author of the popular books *Ingenuity* and *Ingenuity in Practice* and has published his research within leading academic journals such as *Entrepreneurship Theory & Practice, Research Policy, Journal of Management Studies, Academy of Management Learning & Education* and newspapers and periodicals such as the *Washington Post* and the *Financial Times*. He is chair of the award-winning Young Entrepreneurs Schemes that have developed the entrepreneurial skills of more than 5,000 academic researchers. Simon has led innovative training seminars to entrepreneurs and managers based within SMEs, multinational corporations, local government, the public sector and academe across Europe, the USA and Asia and has held research and management posts at BP and Courtaulds.

Hannah Noke is an Associate Professor in Entrepreneurship and Innovation at the University of Nottingham Business School. Her research interests lie in the broad area of entrepreneurship and innovative behaviour, with a particular focus on understanding the early-stage start-up process and how entrepreneurs make sense of opportunities, as well as the entrepreneurial and innovative processes in larger organisations – particularly in public sector organisations. Hannah is the author and co-author of numerous peer-reviewed academic articles in leading UK and European journals and author of a number of book chapters.

Paul Kirkham has been researching and writing in the field of entrepreneurial creativity with the University of Nottingham since 2008. Along with his colleagues Simon Mosey and Martin Binks, he is co-deviser of a problem-solving process, expounded briefly and at length in the books *Ingenuity in Practice* and *Ingenuity*. The Ingenuity Process, developed at the Haydn Green Institute for Innovation and Entrepreneurship, is a guide for clear thinking taught to all Nottingham University Business School students in the UK, China and Malaysia. As part of the university's Executive Education provision, Paul has taught and mentored the process to a wide range of recipients from schools to SMEs and multinational organisations. Recently, his prime concern has been testing and delivering the digital version – Ingenuity Online – to students and businesses right across the globe. Prior to his involvement with the university, Paul worked for many years in the manufacturing sector.

Routledge Masters in Entrepreneurship
Edited by Janine Swail and Robert Wapshott

The **Routledge Masters in Entrepreneurship** series offers postgraduate students specialist but accessible textbooks on a range of entrepreneurship topics. Collectively, these texts form a significant resource base for those studying entrepreneurship, whether as part of an entrepreneurship-related programme of study, or as a new, non-cognate area for students in disciplines such as science and engineering, helping them to gain an in-depth understanding of contemporary entrepreneurial concepts.

The volumes in this series are authored by leading specialists in their field, and although they are discrete texts in their treatment of individual topics, all are united by a common structure and pedagogical approach. Key features of each volume include:

- a critical approach to combining theory with practice, which educates its reader rather than solely teaching a set of skills
- clear learning objectives for each chapter
- the use of figures, tables and boxes to highlight key ideas, concepts and skills
- an annotated bibliography, guiding students in their further reading, and
- discussion questions for each chapter to aid learning and put key concepts into practice.

Resourcing the Start-Up Business
Creating Dynamic Entrepreneurial Learning Capabilities
Oswald Jones, Allan Macpherson and Dilani Jayawarna

Entrepreneurship, Small Business and Public Policy
Evolution and Revolution
Robert J. Bennett

Finance for Small and Entrepreneurial Businesses
Richard Roberts

Managing Human Resources in Small and Medium-Sized Enterprises
Entrepreneurship and the Employment Relationship
Robert Wapshott and Oliver Mallett

Building an Entrepreneurial Organisation
Simon Mosey, Hannah Noke and Paul Kirkham

Building an Entrepreneurial Organisation

Simon Mosey, Hannah Noke
and Paul Kirkham

Routledge
Taylor & Francis Group
LONDON AND NEW YORK

First published 2017
by Routledge
2 Park Square, Milton Park, Abingdon, Oxon OX14 4RN

and by Routledge
711 Third Avenue, New York, NY 10017

Routledge is an imprint of the Taylor & Francis Group, an informa business

© 2017 Simon Mosey, Hannah Noke and Paul Kirkham

The right of Simon Mosey, Hannah Noke and Paul Kirkham to be identified as authors of this work has been asserted by them in accordance with sections 77 and 78 of the Copyright, Designs and Patents Act 1988.

All rights reserved. No part of this book may be reprinted or reproduced or utilised in any form or by any electronic, mechanical, or other means, now known or hereafter invented, including photocopying and recording, or in any information storage or retrieval system, without permission in writing from the publishers.

Trademark notice: Product or corporate names may be trademarks or registered trademarks, and are used only for identification and explanation without intent to infringe.

British Library Cataloguing in Publication Data
A catalogue record for this book is available from the British Library

Library of Congress Cataloging in Publication Data
Names: Mosey, Simon, author. | Noke, Hannah, author. | Kirkham, Paul, author.
Title: Building an entrepreneurial organisation / Simon Mosey, Hannah Noke and Paul Kirkham.
Description: Abingdon, Oxon ; New York, NY : Routledge, 2017.
Identifiers: LCCN 2016045301| ISBN 9781138861138 (pbk.) | ISBN 9781315716084 (e-book) | ISBN 9781138861121 (hbk)
Subjects: LCSH: Creative ability in business. | Entrepreneurship. | Organizational behavior. | New products. | Technological innovations–Management. | Diffusion of innovations–Management.
Classification: LCC HD53 .M676 2017 | DDC 658.4/21–dc23
LC record available at https://lccn.loc.gov/2016045301

ISBN: 978-1-138-86112-1 (hbk)
ISBN: 978-1-138-86113-8 (pbk)
ISBN: 978-1-315-71608-4 (ebk)

Typeset in Bembo
by Cenveo Publisher Services

Contents

List of figures	viii
List of tables	ix
List of cases	x
List of guest contributors	xi
Preface	xii
Acknowledgements	xiii
1 How to build an entrepreneurial organisation	1
2 Entrepreneurial strategy	21
3 Strategy in practice: insights from an entrepreneurial multinational	36
4 Entrepreneurial culture and leadership: structure, processes and people	47
5 Building a culture of entrepreneurship in practice	59
6 Entrepreneurship with external stakeholders	73
7 Managing uncertainty and failure	88
8 Building an ambidextrous organisation	102
9 Diagnosing an entrepreneurial change programme	115
Index	133

Figures

2.1	Adapted from Stevenson and Jarillo's continuum of entrepreneurial management	23
2.2	The financial implications of different types of innovations	28
4.1	The elements of culture within an entrepreneurial organisation	48
4.2	Questioning human resource practices for recruiting and rewarding entrepreneurial behaviours	49
6.1	Summary of Rothwell's five generations of innovation process models	74
6.2	The open innovation approach	76
7.1	Classifying the uncertainty within potential innovation challenges for new products or services	92
8.1	Knowledge transfer practices at Toyota	104
8.2	Absorptive capacity	106

Tables

1.1	Neonatal case innovation challenge: concepts	18
1.2	Neonatal case innovation challenge: potential responses	18
2.1	Percentage return on sales for the automotive industry	29
2.2	ERCC framework showing the paradigm change for Tesla Roadster	31
6.1	Examples of recombinant innovation	76
6.2	How to specify and evaluate an innovation challenge to external stakeholders	78
6.3	Evaluation matrix for external opportunities	82
6.4	One approach to external opportunity evaluation	85
7.1	Questions to test your judgement	90
7.2	Answers to the judgement quiz	91
9.1	Diagnostic framework for entrepreneurial practices	120

Cases

1.1	How innovation really works: 'ready meals'	4
1.2	Neonatal care in the developing world	14
2.1	Football crazy	32
6.1	An exercise in project selection	81
7.1	How innovation really works: almost losing your shirt in the tailoring business	97
8.1	Reconciling learning practices at Disney and Pixar	110
9.1	An example of opportunity-driven entrepreneurship: PureGym	116

Guest contributors

Jim Crilly has more than 30 years' service with one of the largest consumer goods companies in the world: Unilever. Over the years he has held sixteen different job titles across the entire R&D spectrum from basic research as a scientist at the bench through product development and general management before becoming the Senior Vice President for Discover (Research). It is this upstream role which interacts directly with the leading research institutes and universities around the world where new technologies are created and new science is born. Throughout this time Jim has been an active observer and ardent advocate of strategy development and the management of innovation. Furthermore, he has pioneered several projects which have led to the placement of sustainability at the heart of the company's vision. He has been an Honorary Professor in Innovation Management in the School of Bioscience at the University of Nottingham since 2012.

David Falzani started his working life in the electronics industry with IBM and News Corporation before joining a Silicon Valley start-up that grew from 250 to 2,000 employees in two years. David is a Chartered Engineer, gained an MBA attending the Wharton School/SDA Bocconi, has both a certificate and a diploma in company direction from the Institute of Directors and is a Visiting Professor in Sustainable Wealth Creation at Nottingham University Business School. He has been involved in a significant number of entrepreneurial businesses, raising more than £4.5 million of venture capital, the largest round being more than £1 million.

Preface

This book explains how to encourage organisations to be more entrepreneurial. It builds upon our research and teaching experience as we have worked together with enthusiastic colleagues to overcome inappropriate bureaucracy around the world. We show how entrepreneurship can be used to achieve sustainable growth within small firms and to revitalise large firms that have either stagnated or are at risk of failing to realise the potential of new opportunities. By reconciling the two disparate literature streams of entrepreneurship and innovation management we move away from a 'one size fits all' approach towards a more nuanced appreciation of how innovation really works.

Emulating our teaching approach, we draw heavily from case examples of radical innovation across diverse settings: from football to the emergency ward, travelling from Silicon Valley to the British high street. We interview leading practitioners with direct responsibility for building new global brands and growing disruptive technology start-ups and challenge the reader to make entrepreneurial decisions on real life cases and reflect upon those decisions.

The aim is to provide an understanding of entrepreneurship in context, mediated by theory and reinforced through practice. It builds towards a diagnostic tool that can be used to formulate a change in practices for organisations that want to make entrepreneurship central to their culture. Our hope is that the whole should serve as an ideas bank from which appropriate solutions can be drawn, adapted and inspired.

Acknowledgements

The authors would like to thank Margaret Anne Rouse for capturing our lecture transcripts, Catherine Thompson for her edits and Martin Binks for his editing and invaluable suggestions for improving the clarity of the text. We would also like to thank the inspirational undergraduate, masters, MBA students and managers whom we have worked with to hone and refine the material over many years of enjoyable discussion. Finally we would like to thank the editorial team at Routledge for their patience, diligence and support.

1 How to build an entrepreneurial organisation

Simon Mosey and Paul Kirkham

1.1 Introduction

Entrepreneurship and innovation are commonly considered to be exceptional activities carried out by heroic individuals. We contend, however, that successful innovations can be created by any organisation that chooses to make entrepreneurship the 'way we do things around here'. In this chapter we explain how innovation really works from considering prosaic developments such as 'ready meals', through to the life-changing challenges of creating better neonatal incubators. We explain how such innovations are realised by counterintuitive practices such as asking 'what can we do without' and 'what can we do differently'. We conclude by proposing a decision-making approach that any manager can use to examine their own entrepreneurial practices and explore alternative approaches to deliver sustained innovative performance.

1.2 What is an entrepreneurial organisation?

What is an entrepreneurial organisation? We all know what an organisation is and have some idea of what an entrepreneur is, but what makes an entrepreneurial organisation? Because the word *entrepreneur* is associated with individuals, our immediate thoughts about entrepreneurs may be influenced by celebrities such as Richard Branson or Donald Trump and not the organisations they lead. There's no shortage of business people who have become famous as entrepreneurs: retailers; inventors, industrialists like Anita Roddick, James Dyson and Lakshmi Mittal; the techies like Steve Jobs, Bill Gates, Mark Zuckerberg *et al*. They tend to attract (sometimes deliberately) myths around themselves: that they are risk takers; that they are ruthless; that they are lucky; that they are loners – that they are 'special'.

It's all very well to pick and choose favourite individuals but an academic definition needs a little more rigour. Academics, as might be expected, propose different approaches: in the French tradition the entrepreneur is a 'middleman'; in the classic tradition – any business owner; the neo-classical tradition – a rational manager; the Austrian tradition – a radical innovator; the modern

Austrian tradition – a recogniser of opportunities and in the Chicago tradition – a calculated risk taker. And so on.[1]

When we look at the best-known entrepreneurs we find a great variety of often conflicting characteristics: some left school early, others are highly educated; some are technically accomplished, others couldn't mend a fuse; some have narrow expertise, others have broad experience; some are primarily motivated by money, others only want autonomy. It is fair to remark that the famous names are preponderantly white and male.

To reconcile this diversity, modern theoreticians lean towards a behavioural approach – what are the actions that lead to success? And a consensus is emerging that entrepreneurship is concerned with recognising opportunities, coming up with alternatives and choosing the best one.[2]

Economist Joseph Alois Schumpeter is usually held responsible for popularising the word 'entrepreneur'. His entrepreneur identifies and creates opportunities and takes action to realise those new possibilities. And the essence of this definition is action. Once the innovation is established the entrepreneur's role is over.

> everyone is an entrepreneur only when he actually 'carries out new combinations,' and loses that character as soon as he has built up his business, when he settles down to running it as other people run their businesses. This is the rule, of course, and hence it is just as rare for anyone always to remain an entrepreneur throughout the decades of his active life as it is for a businessman never to have a moment in which he is an entrepreneur, to however modest a degree.[3]

Seen this way, concentrating on behaviours – the parts they play rather than the personalities of the actors themselves – it's clear that entrepreneurial thinking need not be limited to superhero individuals. It should rather consider special actions; roles that are taken up for a time and then put down again. And so entrepreneurship can apply to any of us whether as individuals or as organisations or as parts of organisations (regardless incidentally of ethnicity or gender).

To clarify our approach, take this historical example to answer an important question: *is an organisation that is founded by an entrepreneur necessarily entrepreneurial?*

Henry Ford was a dynamic personality who revolutionised the world by putting together his business in an entirely new way, arguably without being responsible for any original invention, certainly neither the motor car nor the assembly line. But does that make the Ford Motor Company an entrepreneurial organisation? The company is still going but the wreckage around it that was once the city of Detroit is a stark reminder that things can go very wrong indeed. It is the ongoing behaviour of the organisation that counts. Many of the most famous entrepreneurs in history did not manage to bequeath an entrepreneurial legacy. Their business empires died with them or, if passed on, failed to survive beyond one generation. On the other hand, as we shall see, certain organisations that have not had an entrepreneurial reputation can make the decision to change. So we will be discussing entrepreneurship rather than entrepreneurs – entrepreneurship as a deliberate action of bringing about innovation, another word which has become very popular, albeit equally contentious.

1.3 Understanding innovation

We live in a world where innovation seems more important than ever before. Whether used in promoting the latest technology or being included in the mission statements of organisations from multinational manufacturers to financial services to the public sector, the word is everywhere. And yet there was a time when innovation was not very popular as a concept. The mere idea of doing things differently has been regarded with suspicion for most of human history. Most people were content to do more or less exactly as their forebears had done: change was seen as a dangerous novelty. By the twentieth century, however, innovation had come to be seen as the driving force of economic development, a bright hope, to be encouraged rather than resisted. And so nowadays innovation is omnipresent, there are government departments for innovation, and it is generally thought of as a good thing.

Canadian academic Benoît Godin puts it thus:

> A firm cannot ignore investing in innovation or, if ignored, it pretends it does innovate.[4]

How much of the rhetoric of innovation is 'lip-service' remains debatable. But most organisations and businesses seem to want innovation, and many have departments and individuals specifically tasked to be responsible for innovation. However, a 2013 survey of organisations with revenues exceeding £80 million shows that although 'the vast majority of executives (93 percent) continue to regard their company's long-term success to be dependent on its ability to innovate', 'at the same time less than one out of five (18 percent) believe their own innovation strategy is delivering a competitive advantage.'[5]

As we shall see in Chapter 2, this presents a challenge for those of us in the innovation business. The fact that the demand for innovation is not being satisfied, even in the largest organisations – those which have devoted time and resources for it – suggests that the whole area is not very well understood, that effort may be being misdirected and even counter-productive.

When asked what innovation means and what they want from it, people give widely differing and uncertain responses:

> There are ideas around creativity; about creating something new, maybe a product or maybe a process. There are ideas around making life simpler – inventing or discovering something that makes it easier or makes it better.

So innovation could be about improvement.

In business it could be making yourself stand out and gaining a competitive advantage.[6]

It may then be a matter of maintaining the position that you have in the market. And there is a difference between line extensions and step changes; disruptive innovations that threaten the status quo.

So there is the idea of innovation as an entrepreneurial tool.[7]

Another aspect is that we have to react to new inventions or discoveries – innovation as imitation, a process of keeping up, a fear of being left behind.[8]

And in opposition to the idea of progress, and of progress being inevitable, is the attitude that 'if it ain't broke, why try to fix it'.

We can see a few key words emerging: creativity, invention, discovery, improvement, disruption, which we need to pick apart if we are to understand the dynamics of innovation and therefore entrepreneurial action.

Clearly innovation is about change but sometimes it is unclear exactly what has changed. See, for example, the following case study.

CASE 1.1 HOW INNOVATION REALLY WORKS: 'READY MEALS'

Consider the following somewhat puzzling piece of news:

> Sales of luxury ready meals from the chilled cabinet in many UK supermarkets actually rose during the financial crisis of 2008 onwards. A very basic understanding of markets would lead one to expect luxury items to be the first to feel the pinch in straightened times.

The explanation comes when we look at the question from a different point of view; the real competition for ready meals of this type is clear in some promotional copy: 'dine in for £10'. The prime competitor is the restaurant - a 'luxury' night in is more economical than a cheap night out or even a takeaway meal.

It is possible to speculate that the dominance of chilled foods in the UK is the result of the success of one entrepreneurial supermarket, Marks & Spencer, introducing a new category – the luxury chilled meal – which was itself arguably a response to image problems caused by the move to manufacturing their clothes range overseas. As an organisation, Marks & Spencer also pioneered the concept of 'luxury' chilled supermarket food items in the UK with the 'Chicken Kiev', first introduced in 1979 (priced at £1.99 for two). The origins of the recipe are disputed amongst chefs, yet Marks &

Spencer clearly paid no royalties to any inventor before 'launching' their 'new' product. Equally, rival supermarkets paid no royalties to Marks & Spencer as they quickly developed their own versions. The changing fortunes of the Kiev in recent times can be regarded as a convenient marker of a change in consumer attitudes. Economies of scale and competition from other retailers have meant that the price has not risen significantly despite nearly 40 years of inflation. And so what was seen as a 'dining out' experience at home has been devalued almost to junk-food status and replaced by more complex 'gourmet' collections that all UK supermarkets now offer with very little distinction between them.

Interestingly, the meteoric growth of the chilled food sector was not driven by new practices in supermarket marketing, as is commonly assumed. The enabling innovations came from somewhere else – developments in IT which revolutionised supply-chain logistics and enabled 'just in time' delivery of more perishable items.[9]

So instead of a nice neat chain of cause and effect, we see a complex web of players with different agendas, organisations making short-term gains enabled by innovations 'borrowed' from elsewhere.

There are some who conclude that innovation is inherently muddled and unpredictable, for example, British geneticist Professor Steve Jones stated:

> Innovation is an entirely random process. Planning and innovation are entirely opposed to each other so anybody who thinks they can plan what can be discovered next is wasting their time.[10]

Presumably Jones is defending the intangible benefits of pure 'blue sky' research and yet many organisations do plan innovation – and some do so very effectively indeed. Many use the term 'organised chaos' to describe the process.

This book aims towards a better understanding of innovation than surrendering it to pure chance. We offer an explanation of what it means, how it works and the forces resisting it; we use this understanding to offer a mechanism to build an entrepreneurial organisation.

1.4 Definitions of innovation

Thousands of books and papers have been written about innovation, yet many of them have no agreed-on or even working definitions.

Part of the confusion arises from the interchangeable uses of the terms *invention*, *innovation*, *creativity* and *design* (and that's just in English). To an extent they share common themes: novelty, utility and change. As we have noted, in recent times and with significant exceptions change is usually, even when it is disruptive, thought of as 'change for the better'.

For clarity, we are going to assume the following working definitions:[11]

Discovery is the detection or unearthing of new knowledge.

Creativity is the generation of new ideas, usually as a response to perceived problems and opportunities.

Invention and design are the engineering of new ideas and discoveries into viable products, shaping them into practical and attractive propositions for end-users – creativity deployed to a specific end.

Innovation is the successful exploitation of new ideas. It is the process that carries ideas into actions, be they new manufacturers or services or technologies; new organisations and businesses; new ways of organising and doing business, even new ways of thinking. The essence of innovation is action, it is the bringing of value and doing things differently. Novelty for its own sake without bringing value, or paying lip-service whilst not actually doing anything differently, is not innovation.

Take genetic fingerprinting and the fact that variations in DNA are unique to individuals. This discovery sparked the creativity of researchers leading to the invention and design of various applications which have had revolutionary consequences in totally unrelated fields from medicine to law. Another example is the man-made substance graphene, a crystalline form of carbon only one atom thick. Its unique characteristics have vast potential in an even wider range of applications. We see a progression from discovery to invention and design leading to potential innovation.

1.5 Different forms of innovation

Different forms of innovation can be distinguished; these are rarely if ever clearly delineated, and any particular innovation may feature more than one. Joe Tidd and John Bessant[12] differentiate four types of innovation:

1. Product Innovation – changes in products or services that an organisation offers.
2. Process Innovation – changes in the way that products or services are created and delivered.
3. Position Innovation – changes in the context in which products or services are introduced.
4. Paradigm Innovation – changes in the underlying mental models which frame organisations' activities.

The iPad was a new product; 3D printing is a new process; budget airlines represent a change of market position; microwave cookery was a new paradigm (that is, something that had not been done before).

Henry Ford's organisation managed to innovate in all four areas. The Ford Motor company offered a new product, the Model T; manufactured using a new process, the assembly line; to a new position, the mass market, which changes several paradigms at once, not least in employment practices: his workers were also prospective customers.

Tidd and Bessant suggest that there are two very simple questions any would-be innovator should ask:
'*What can we do better?*'
'*What can we do differently?*'
An example could be as simple as moving from payment by cash to payment by card (better) as opposed to payment by mobile phone (different).

1.6 Incremental and radical innovation

Tidd and Bessant's questions illustrate another important distinction, that is, between incremental and radical innovation. As a rule of thumb radical innovations cannot be tracked back to a previous version. The recorded-music industry supplies good examples: the MP3 player has no roots in the technology of the tape cassette; the vinyl disc is an improvement on the shellac disc whereas the compact disc is not. Radical innovations tend to disrupt and destroy older ways of doing things in a process that Schumpeter called *creative destruction*.

But the distinction depends upon your point of view; some radical innovations have little discernible effect on users, such as changing 'copper' coins to ferrous. Similarly, the 'just-in-time' production and supply that we saw in the 'ready-meals' food market is a radical process innovation that goes by almost unnoticed by consumers. On the other hand, some seemingly incremental innovations can have radical consequences. For example, most of us would recognise the e-reader as a radical innovation in publishing and would think of the paperback as merely an incremental improvement in manufacture. And yet the paperback had radical consequences, opening up an entirely new market in the same way the printing press did hundreds of years earlier.

Incremental innovations tend to be new products and processes; radical ones tend to bring new positions and paradigms. In sum, incremental innovation improves – radical innovation transforms, often as a response to a new problem or a new opportunity, often coming from outside existing practice: movie studios were never going to invent online streaming. Radical innovation does not have to be earth shattering but it does have to be different. It may only be 'new to me' or 'new to the organisation' but it has to bring value to however modest a degree. Schumpeter emphasises 'Innovation is possible without anything we should identify as invention, and invention does not necessarily induce innovation.' His point of view is that of business; therefore, innovation is 'The action of introducing a new product into the market; a product newly brought on to the market'. To address the challenge of inclusivity, he makes the definition even looser: 'any "doing things differently" in the realm of economic life'.[13]

1.7 Reconciling entrepreneurship and innovation

Although there is a common theme, note the subtle distinction between innovation and entrepreneurship – the latter is far more opportunistic and disruptive; the value brought is often value shifted from the old to the new without much sensitivity or delicacy. We reconcile the two definitions within an organisational context by proposing that an entrepreneurial organisation is one that develops innovations that create new value and are new to the organisation.

The value is not necessarily financial; it might be increased knowledge, it might be increased efficiency, it might be decreased waste or decreased crime or sickness. It could even be increased happiness, but for most organisations it should eventually show up in the bottom line. The terminology of business is useful to describe innovation in all fields. All new ways of doing things find themselves in a marketplace of end-users, who will make choices as to whether they like them or not. The value brought could be short lived: as long as it repays the investment it ought to be regarded as a success. Innovation is not necessarily interested in the long term.

This 'doing differently' occurs against a background of 'business as usual' – the nuts and bolts of managing any enterprise.

'Business as usual' can be planned for and managed using discounted cash flow, expected rate of return and net present value models – all essential tools that business schools have been very good at teaching over the last hundred years or so.[14] Such approaches work well when the external environment changes only slowly and predictably whilst the internal environment, the firm itself, is equally homogenous. Nowadays, however, as we see every day when we switch on the news, the external environment is complex and fast moving. Consumer demands, technology, politics, the economic system itself, are all changing at an ever-increasing rate. VUCA is the fashionable acronym used to capture such volatility, uncertainty, complexity and ambiguity. Certainly, it is much more difficult to forecast long-term external change. And it is equally difficult to deal with internal change: most organisations are not as homogenous and predictable as they used to be. People who join a big corporation, work for that corporation all their life and then retire are the exception rather than the rule. In Chapters 3 and 5 we will hear the views of one such exceptional individual who has held 16 different entrepreneurial roles in the multinational consumer goods organisation Unilever. In Chapter 3, he shares his experiences of developing an entrepreneurial strategy to address disruptive changes in consumer behaviour alongside the challenge of extending the organisation's competencies through alliances and new business development. In Chapter 5 he explains the contribution of entrepreneurial leadership and culture to deliver their entrepreneurial strategy and achieve sustained innovative performance.

Although the traditional planning tools have stood the test of time, as Unilever concluded, they are now less relevant. Many smaller fast-moving firms have grown globally in a short space of time while not working in the ways of the past: they, and their employees, are working in a very different way – flexible and fast moving. How can we reconcile the predictability of the past with an understanding of future uncertainty?

Entrepreneurial analysis offers a greater understanding of how innovation happens. Thinking back to the ready meals example in Case 1.1, we can see that links of cause and effect make an irregular, sometimes confused and tangled net. A more detailed critique of the still dominant linear models of innovation is discussed in Chapter 6.

But we haven't answered the question of why it happens: what are the driving forces of innovation?

1.8 Why does innovation happen?

A body of evidence supports the thesis that innovation arises as a result of a crisis. It is argued that the advances in animal husbandry, plant breeding and agricultural machinery were all born as a response to the crisis of population growth.[15] But, as Norman Borlaug, awarded the Nobel Peace Prize for his part in agricultural research, pointed out thirty years on: 'Mushrooming populations, changing demographics and inadequate poverty intervention programs have eaten up many of the gains of the Green Revolution.'[16] It may be worth remembering that some more contemporary advances are contested, for example the shale-gas-extraction technique known as 'fracking': is it proof of our ability to innovate ourselves out of a problem, or is it a 'get out of jail free card' which does not address the root cause?

So, is crisis the imperative? Another celebrated Nobel laureate, Milton Friedman, thought so:

> Only a crisis—actual or perceived—produces real change.[17]

But using the word 'only' is palpable nonsense.

It is no exaggeration to suggest that the smart phone may be the enabling technology that transforms the developing world. In the 1990s it was widely asserted that half the world's population had never made a phone call. And yet twenty years later two-thirds of the population of Africa had phones of their own![18] The world is becoming connected through mobile devices – real change, unrelated to crisis. There was no crisis in communication in the 1990s that forced people to develop mobile phone technology. Instead, it was opportunity which was the driving force of change, and the capacity to produce ever-cheaper models which created the mass market. The same can be seen with many other world-shattering innovations, from the printing press to the motor car – even the chicken Kiev![19] In Chapter 6, we will therefore explore different approaches to opportunity recognition, ranging from organisations working with extreme users wanting a better product to ingenious managers recombining well-established, existing ideas from across the organisation.

Crisis does of course bring change if only because crises tend to be situations in which staying the same is not an option. The pace has become so fast that most of us have to get used to doing things differently on a regular basis, whether we like it or not. So much so that we seem to be living in a state of near-permanent crisis, which might explain all the talk of innovation.

Both crisis and opportunity have a part to play – in certain circumstances they might be seen as two sides of the same coin, but not always; sometimes one person's crisis is another's opportunity. For instance, the crisis faced by video-rental companies due to peer-to-peer video sharing was an opportunity for video-streaming providers. Yet sometimes the opportunity causes the crisis; Uber's exploitation of peer-to-peer communication between customers and potential drivers created a crisis amongst taxi drivers. Friedman's optimism is directed more to the opportunist than the incumbent. It's all part of Schumpeter's gale of creative destruction. And of course the situation for organisations is even more complicated since the crises/opportunities can be internal as well as external. For Schumpeter it is the response that matters – it can be 'adaptive', building on existing practice, or 'creative', overturning existing practice. For Schumpeter the 'creative response is an essential element in the historical process'[20] and it is in the reaction to the problems of crisis and opportunity that we see entrepreneurial practices as key drivers of innovation. Understanding how to build an environment within organisations in which such practices can flourish is the principal purpose of this text.

1.9 Understanding organisational change

So how does a better understanding of innovation help organisations rather than individuals? As we saw with entrepreneurs, the temptation is to define innovative organisations by specific examples that always seem to be ahead of the game and ask the question 'why can't we be more like them?' So a common first response is to choose one and try to do what they do. There is nothing inherently wrong with straightforward imitation; indeed, intriguing evidence suggests that imitation is an extremely effective social learning strategy, but it is risky and out of your control.[21] What if you had imitated the 'rank and yank' practices of the firm named by *Fortune* magazine as 'America's Most Innovative Company' for six years running? That company was Enron; its shareholders lost $74 billion, and the president was sent to prison for 24 years.

So, once we have disregarded the crooks, how can we judge which examples to follow? Both Apple and Google are regularly cited as the most innovative companies around and their product range and share price would seem to bear this out. But if we were writing this book a few years ago we might have cited MySpace and AltaVista. With all due respect to the present-day tech giants, although they are admirable examples of high-growth entrepreneurship they have yet to prove themselves sustainable.

More important, and as we saw with individual entrepreneurs, many of the most successful companies are fundamentally different in their approach and culture. It would seem that for every firm that is innovative in one way there is at least one other being just as successful doing it completely differently. For every open-desk policy there seems to be a skunkworks just around the corner. While one person is busy gold-plating their service, elsewhere someone is stripping theirs to the essentials. Should innovation be in-house or should we embrace open-source? Should we judge a firm as innovative because of the number of patents it holds? How is it possible to measure innovations that are trade secrets? All these approaches seem valid, and we will discuss them in more detail in Chapters 4 through Chapter 6.

And again we will look at general behaviours more than specific cases. Those behaviours change over time.

There is a remarkable similarity among models of change in economics (Schumpeter), business (Utterback & Abernathy, Martin), management (March), science (Kuhn, Mokyr) and evolution (Eldredge & Gould).[22]

All these distinguish between two phases in the lifetime of anything new: creative/adaptive; exploration/exploitation; heuristic/algorithmic; product/process; revolutionary/normal; macroinvention/microinvention – the words are different but they all describe the same phenomenon: radical change followed by incremental change. If we use the language of business, a new product or service is introduced and then the production/delivery process is honed and refined over time. Process innovation is easy to measure, and its efficiency is reinforced by 'predictable' success – the bottom line. Most of us find certainty more comfortable than risk. Any entity which is doing well and improving measurably will see no reason to change unless forced to, and that is always likely to be sub-optimal for the organisation. Managing and balancing the resulting tensions within the organisation is the subject of Chapter 8.

Organisations of all kinds can go through several 'lifetimes' as they grow; the processes which make them successful at one stage threaten them at the next. At such a point carrying on in the same old way is no longer an option. The crisis is internal and the option is 'innovate or die'. And this is true from the sole trader physically unable to work any harder to the multimillion-pound enterprise striving to keep up with demand; if they want to grow they will have to change. It might be as small as taking on one new employee or as large as launching a public company but the practices will need to change nonetheless.

Individuals, organisations and institutions delivering/servicing any innovation almost inevitably become less open and more risk averse over time. The irony is that whilst we stand in awe of grand long-running institutions and feel that they must be in control of the long view, in fact they often become more and more short term in behaviour. With the consequence that, like the dodo (which was perfectly adapted to its environment), they become more and more susceptible to the other type of crisis, external disruptive innovation, at the very time when they have most to lose. In 1972 American academic Larry Greiner devised a growth model elucidating these crisis points as

> a series of developmental phases through which companies tend to pass as they grow. Each phase begins with a period of evolution, with steady growth and stability, and ends with a revolutionary period of substantial organizational turmoil and change—for instance, when centralized practices eventually lead to demands for decentralization. The resolution of each revolutionary period determines whether or not a company will move forward into its next stage of evolutionary growth.[23]

As Greiner points out, 'the logic of paradox underlying the model continues to ring true, although it often haunts and confuses the managerial psyche. Managers have difficulty in understanding that an organizational solution introduced by them personally in one phase eventually sows the seeds of revolution.'[24] This is true of some very big names, even when they see it coming; both Kodak and Sony were caught out by digital technologies that they themselves had been instrumental in developing. With hindsight, and with sweeping generalisation, Kodak could be said to have led innovation in the first three Ps listed above – developing new products and processes and creating new market positions – but they failed to cope with the changing paradigm. Their business had always been heavily reliant upon selling film for cameras, so printing at home on a PC took away one of their prime sources of revenue.

1.10 Determining innovation challenges

For a manager attempting to plan for the inevitable need to change, it can be helpful to consider another distinction between the drivers of change – some are internal, others are external.

Internal innovation challenges include:

- innovation for growth – most new or growing businesses are offering a new proposition
- innovation as a consequence of growth – as an enterprise grows it is just not possible to carry on as before; at its simplest there are not enough hours in the day – something has to change
- to maintain/increase competitive edge – innovation to stay ahead of the game.

External innovation challenges result from:

- a response to competition
- a response to new technology
- new discoveries
- new regulations
- new fashions
- new trends
- new markets
- booms and busts – unexpected changes in the economic cycle
- international factors – wars and natural disasters.

The first list is short but is inevitable and therefore to a large extent predictable. The second list is longer but is not inevitable; nor is it predictable – we may get lucky!

The overall challenge, then, is to maintain the spirit of renewal between the intrinsic crisis points so that innovation can be planned rather than forced; each challenge can be seen as an opportunity. Those buzzwords 'agility' and 'resilience' are most appropriate to the unpredictable challenges. And the truly entrepreneurial organisation is the one which deliberately seeks them out. Some organisations consistently disrupt from within; for example, Bell Laboratories oversaw several paradigm shifts – from valves to transistors to electronics and to satellites. Others deliberately change their behaviour; for example, Proctor & Gamble consciously adopted a radically different approach to R&D (research and development). Neither is such an initiative limited to private business – public bodies such as the British Police and National Health Services have shown an interest in new ways of thinking. Institutions like governments, schools and hospitals have all innovated over the years, despite significant resistance to change, so there are lessons to learn – it can be done. We will be looking at this in more detail in Chapter 4.

Dealers in FMCGs (fast-moving consumer goods) have to innovate all the time and we will study their practices through the example of Unilever in Chapters 3 and 5. The 3M Company is also a well-known exemplar of innovation and we will examine it briefly in Chapter 9.

But as a long list of famous but defunct names attests, eminence and longevity are not enough – in business, past performance is no indicator of future prospects. And so it is instructive to look at some of the casualties and some of the survivors: Back in the 1960s two of the most popular playthings in Britain were construction toys: Airfix and Meccano. Now they are remembered nostalgically and occupy niche markets whereas fifty years later their upstart Danish rival Lego was selling in more than 130 countries with consistent year-on-year growth in double figures. We will examine the remarkable durability of Lego in Chapter 6.

Another related example: what does the cash security specialist De La Rue PLC have in common with the Nintendo Corporation? Answer: although they have tried a lot of things since, when they began the core business of both companies was manufacturing playing cards. De La Rue's best innovations were down the path of high-quality printing to banknotes and postage stamps; Nintendo's were toys and games. We will look at the development of such core competencies and how they can be extended or replaced in Chapter 2.

So 'distance of travel' may be a positive indicator – it is possible to be innovative in a fast-moving domain without moving from the core business. Take the example of a high-street music shop such as HMV. Founded in the nineteenth century, it first sold instruments and sheet music, then moved into wax cylinders, vinyl discs, tape, cassettes, CDs, even MP3 players before finally being rendered obsolete by the online innovations of Amazon and Apple.

In this case, there has been lots of innovation in products and plenty in processes (cash registers, computerised stock control etc.) but precious little in position and virtually zero in paradigm. The old way of doing things doesn't work anymore: there is a clear need for new business models. The British high street is in a state of flux – a fine example of crisis and opportunity. On the crisis side, there are empty units, charity shops, pawnbrokers and bookmakers. But on the opportunity side there are pop-up arts and music shows, coffee shops and late-night convenience stores (often operated by the retail chains whose out-of-town supermarkets contributed to the demise of the old model!). Most interesting is the repurposing of the high street – a paradigm shift, a change in the mental model of what a high street is for. Many consumers appear to see it as somewhere to occasionally visit for items that cannot be ordered effectively online. By contrast, entrepreneurial retailers are enticing certain consumers back through offering a new mental model; the high street as a luxury social experience that the virtual world cannot yet compete with.

We will consider the very different decision-making approaches that are necessary when you are in the midst of a paradigm change in Chapter 7, but first let's try to deal with a genuine crisis.

For managers faced with the dilemma of knowing that their organisational practices have to change but are unsure what to change and how to do so, the following case study illustrates our approach. Researchers considering decision making with such high degrees of uncertainly argue for the need for case-based reasoning (see Courtney, Lovallo & Clarke, 2013, for a refresher). Here managers should first categorise the root cause of the innovation challenge facing them and then seek analogous solutions to such a challenge. These analogues could be practices from other organisations or from past experiences but the key point is that they then need to be translated so that they will be effective within the new organisational context. This is best illustrated by first practising the approach on someone else's innovation challenge by undertaking the following example, as given in the *New York Times* (see Case 1.2).

CASE 1.2 NEONATAL CARE IN THE DEVELOPING WORLD[25]

Dr. Kristian Olson states the innovation challenge succinctly, relating his experience (in 2008) of an incident on a trip to Cut Nyak Dhien Hospital, a one-story concrete building in the tsunami-stricken city of Meulaboh, Indonesia:

> 'When I walked in the incubator room, a whole family was sobbing around a crib.' Their 7-day-old baby boy, who was born slightly underweight and suffering from infection, had just died, after lying for hours on a cold cot. With warmth and proper care, he would have survived. Crowding the room were six donated high-tech incubators from the West. None of them worked.

According to a 2007 study from Duke University in North Carolina, 96 percent of foreign-donated medical equipment fails within five years of donation — mostly because of electrical problems, like voltage surges or cutbacks (brownouts) or broken switches, or because of training problems, such as neglecting to send user manuals along with the devices.

In the developing world, spare parts and trained technicians are hard to find outside major cities. Regular maintenance of incubators is difficult and even inexpensive parts are unobtainable; for example, researchers found a broken incubator in Katmandu that needed a specific fuse costing US$0.60 – a part the hospital technician hoped to find on his semi-annual trip to Delhi.

Questions

Bearing in mind Tidd and Bessant's possibilities for innovation in product, process, position or paradigm:

- What is the innovation challenge?
- Why doesn't the existing solution work?
- What can be done?

Answers

Supplying low-cost incubators to the developing world is an innovation which has failed. A successful product has been introduced to a new position where it has not thrived for a variety of reasons: it is an expensive product without adequate support in an unsuitable environment. Here are three more appropriate responses:

Solution one: NeoNurture[26]

Innovation challenge – no supply chain

Solution – hijack someone else's supply chain

Make an incubator out of car parts – lights, air filters, thermostats, etc. – and then they can be repaired by local auto mechanics.

In his discussions with doctors who practise in impoverished settings, Dr. Jonathan Rosen of Boston's Center for Integration of Medicine & Innovative Technology (CIMIT) learned that no matter how remote the locale, there always seemed to be a Toyota 4Runner in working order. It was his 'Aha!' moment, he recalled later: 'Why not make the incubator out of new or used car parts, and teach local auto mechanics to be medical technologists?' CIMIT then hired Design That Matters, a nonprofit firm in Cambridge, Mass., to design the machine. Timothy Prestero, the firm's founder and chief executive, recalls: 'The idea was to start with a 4Runner and take away all the parts that weren't an incubator.'

They did not restrict themselves to Toyotas. 'I don't know where you get a replacement incubator filter in a remote Nepalese village, but you likely can find someone there who can replace a car's air filter. That's where this idea really has virtue.'

The NeoNurture incubator takes advantage of two abundant local resources in developing countries: car parts and the knowledge of auto technicians. It leverages the existing supply chain of the auto industry and the technical understanding of local car mechanics. Among other components, it uses sealed-beam headlights as a heating element, a dashboard fan provides convective heat circulation, signal lights and a door chime serve as alarms, and a motorcycle battery and car cigarette lighter provide backup power during incubator transport and power outages.

Future challenges

The car parts incubator has received $150,000 in initial financing from CIMIT. The project team is looking for foundation support to develop a working prototype. Because it does not rely on original products or processes, the incubator will most likely not be patented, though Massachusetts General Hospital (Dr. Olson's home institution) and Design That Matters will share intellectual property rights. But, says Mr Prestero: 'The technology is the least difficult part of the problem. Manufacturing, financing, distribution, regulatory approval: those are major barriers. There aren't many examples of a successfully scaled product to serve the poor.'

Solution two: Kangaroo Care[27]

Innovation challenge – inappropriate technology

Solution – appropriate technology

Skin-to-skin contact with the human body is better than any machine so why not use family members as incubators?

Kangaroo care is a technique practiced on newborn, often premature infants. It seeks to provide restored closeness of the newborn with mother or father by placing the infant in direct skin-to-skin contact with one of them. This ensures physiological and psychological warmth and bonding. The kangaroo position is ideal for feeding. The parent's stable body temperature helps to regulate the newborn's temperature more smoothly than an incubator.

The technique was developed in the mid-1980s by neonatologists Edgar Rey and Hector Martinez in Bogota, Colombia, in response to shortages of power and reliable equipment. They reported a falling mortality rate from 70% to 30%.

Dr. Stephen Wall, a senior research adviser at Save the Children, says global health practitioners should promote the practice more strongly before endorsing new devices like NeoNurture. He notes that most babies in the developing world are born not in hospitals but at home: 'For now, there's an urgent need to provide simple solutions that can be used by families, information that can be shared through community health workers, women's groups or other community mechanisms.'

Kangaroo Care challenges the developed world's tendency for intervention and technological solutions – innovation is a two-way street. In December 2014, NIHCE (the National Institute for Health and Care Excellence) admitted that most babies are better off being born at home.[28]

Solution three: MOM[29]

Innovation challenge – incubators cost thousands of pounds

Solution – make them for £250 each, including delivery

MOM is an inexpensive, electronically controlled, inflatable incubator that can run on car batteries and complies with British incubation standards. It can easily be collapsed and placed into already utilised care packages for easy delivery and transport to refugee camps. The modular nature of the design means separate pieces can be sent for repair if required.

James Roberts of Loughborough University developed the original idea; he was the 2014 winner of the James Dyson Award (winning a £30,000 grant).

1.11 Conclusion – A contingency approach to innovation

Surely the neonatal care innovation challenge is big enough to warrant multiple solutions. Dr. Renée Van de Weerdt, chief of maternal, newborn and child health at UNICEF (The United Nations Children's Emergency Fund) says 'The bottom line is yes, we need more simple technologies in hospitals for the complicated cases. At the same time, we need to accelerate efforts to get skin-to-skin care more widely used for the non-complicated cases.'[30]

Interestingly this comment can be seen against a background of criticism in the developed world of the over-medicalisation of natural processes. In Britain, NIHCE has recognised that home birth is the safest option in uncomplicated cases.[31] And this is also reflected in the results for these three initiatives:

As of 2016, MOM is still looking for investors and sponsors to make the project a reality.[32]

NeoNurture, despite massive acclamation and awards, failed to launch. The developers think the reason is that while they paid a lot of attention to the end

18   *Building an Entrepreneurial Organisation*

users, perhaps they did not engage with existing manufacturers and purchasers to the same extent.[33]

Kangaroo Care, which appears to be the simplest solution, is the one that is actually saving lives on a daily basis and is being credited with reducing infant mortality by one-third.[34]

Note that each of these responses illustrates different approaches to different root causes. MOM addresses the innovation challenge of expense by 'doing better' on price – a product innovation. NeoNurture tackles the spare-part supply chain by 'doing differently' - a process innovation. These approaches also echo Tidd and Bessant's questions. Kangaroo care challenges the dominant paradigm and adds an important new category of 'doing without' – so-called 'frugal innovation'.[35] We plot these different innovation challenges in Table 1.1.

This is not how these particular innovations arose, but the chart shows how they fit in a framework of possibilities for this situation. Such a chart leaves six empty places – let us see if we can fill them with six other potential responses in Table 1.2.

And so we see that a structured approach to innovation can quite quickly suggest a range of possibilities. In this case there are nine answers, each of which may be 'correct', that is, appropriate in this organisational context.

In Chapter 9 we will propose a similar matrix to diagnose and address the entrepreneurial status of any given organisation by considering current entrepreneurial practices and proposing different innovation challenges for how they could be enhanced, removed or replaced.

Table 1.1 Neonatal case innovation challenge: concepts

Root causes	What can we do better?	What can we do without?	What can we do differently?
No on-going support	?	?	NeoNurture
Inappropriate technology	?	Kangaroo Care	?
Too expensive	MOM – value for money	?	?

Table 1.2 Neonatal case innovation challenge: potential responses

Root causes	What can we do better?	What can we do without?	What can we do differently?
No on-going support	Individual ownership of equipment with training	Modular design – fewer replaceable elements	NeoNurture
Inappropriate technology	Mobile self-sufficient clinic	Kangaroo Care	Wind-up generator
Too expensive	MOM – value for money	Shared ownership between clinics	Guaranteed service – 'a bag-for-life'

Our studies will show that there is no single 'correct' answer to the question 'what makes an entrepreneurial organisation?' Our structured, interrogative analysis will result in a multiplicity of alternatives. The following chapters will highlight different areas where firms commonly underperform at innovation and suggest some of the alternative entrepreneurial practices available to answer the slightly different question of: *how can we make your organisation more entrepreneurial?*

References

1 Westhead, P. & Wright, M. (2013). *Entrepreneurship: A Very Short Introduction*. Oxford: Oxford University Press.
2 Kirkham, P., Mosey, S. & Binks, M. (2011). *Ingenuity in Practice: A Guide for Clear Thinking*. Nottingham: University of Nottingham.
3 Schumpeter, J. A. (1912/1934). *The Theory of Economic Development*. New Brunswick, NJ: Transaction Publishers.
4 Those interested in the history of innovation as a concept are directed to the many fascinating papers B. Godin has posted online at www.csiic.ca/.
5 Koetzier, W. & A. Alon (2013). 'Why "low risk" innovation is costly: Overcoming the perils of renovation and invention' at www.accenture.com/SiteCollectionDocuments/PDF/Accenture-Why-Low-Risk-Innovation-Costly.pdf.
6 Readers may be interested in the works of Michael Porter, from the Harvard Business School.
7 Peter Drucker has explored this extensively. See Drucker, P. (1985). *Innovation and Entrepreneurship: Practice and Principles*. New York: Harper & Row.
8 *Disruptive innovation* is the term coined by Clayton Christensen and explored in *The Innovator's Dilemma: When New Technologies Cause Great Firms to Fail* (1997). Cambridge, Mass.: Harvard Business Review Press.
9 Cox, H., Mowatt, S. & Prevezer, M. (2002). 'From frozen fishfingers to chilled chicken tikka: Organisational responses to technical change in the late twentieth century'. Working Paper for the Centre for International Business Studies, London South Bank University.
10 *New Scientist* 26/02/2011.
11 Royal Academy of Engineering (2012). 'Educating engineers to drive the innovation economy'. Available at www.raeng.org.uk/news/publications/list/reports/Innovation_Economy_2012.pdf.
12 Tidd, J. & Bessant, J. (2009). *Managing Innovation: Integrating Technological, Market and Organizational Change*, 4e. Hoboken, NJ: Wiley.
13 Schumpeter, J. A. (1939) *Business Cycles*. New York: McGraw-Hill. (All of the quotations in this paragraph are from Schumpeter.)
14 Courtney, H., Lovallo, D. & Clarke, C. (2013). 'Deciding how to decide: A toolkit for executives making high risk strategic bets'. *Harvard Business Review*.
15 Harari, Y. (2011). *Sapiens: A Brief History of Humankind*. London: Vintage.
16 'The green revolution revisited and the road ahead'. (26 September 2002). Speech to the Nobel Institute. The full text can be found at: www.nobelprize.org/nobel_prizes/peace/laureates/1970/borlaug-lecture.pdf.
17 Friedman, M. (1962). *Capitalism and Freedom*. Chicago: University of Chicago Press.
18 http://guardian.ng/technology/africas-mobile-phone-penetration-now-67/.
19 Schmookler, J. (1966). *Invention and Economic Growth*. Cambridge, Mass.: Harvard University Press.

20 Schumpeter, J. A. (1947). 'The creative response in economic history'. *Journal of Economic History*, 7(2): 149–159.
21 The Social Learning Strategies Tournament was a fascinating experiment conducted by Cultaptation, a research project in the area of dynamics and adaptation in human cumulative culture. See www.intercult.su.se/cultaptation/tournament.php.
22 Readers can explore these by consulting this reading list (presented here alphabetically): Eldredge, N. & Gould, S. J. (1972). 'Punctuated equilibria: An alternative to phyletic gradualism', pp. 82–115 in *Models in Paleobiology*, ed. by T.J.M Schopf. San Francisco: Freeman, Cooper & Co.; Kuhn, T. (1962). *The Structure of Scientific Revolutions*. Chicago: University of Chicago Press; March, J. G. (1991). *Exploration and Exploitation in Organizational Learning*, pubsonline.informs.org; Martin, R., (2009). *The Design of Business*. Cambridge, Mass.: Harvard Business Press; Schumpeter, J. A. (1934). *The Theory of Economic Development*; Utterback, J. M. & Abernathy, W. J. (1975). 'A dynamic model of process and product innovation', *Omega*, 3(6), 639–656.
23 Greiner, L. E. (1972/1998). 'Evolution and revolution as organizations grow'. *Harvard Business Review*. See https://hbr.org/1998/05/evolution-and-revolution-as-organizations-grow.
24 Ibid.
25 See www.nytimes.com/2008/12/16/health/16incubators.html?pagewanted=all&_r=0.
26 See www.designthatmatters.org/neonurture/.
27 Whitelaw A. & Sleath, K. (1985). 'Myth of the marsupial mother: Home care of very low birth weight babies in Bogota, Colombia', *Lancet*. May 25;1(8439): 1206–1208.
28 See www.nice.org.uk/news/article/midwife-led-units-safest-for-straightforward-births.
29 See www.jamesdysonaward.org/projects/mom/.
30 Quoted in the *New York Times*: www.nytimes.com/2008/12/16/health/16incubators.html.
31 See www.theguardian.com/society/2014/dec/03/hospital-childbirth-misconception-home-reversing-nice-guidelines.
32 See www.momincubators.com/contact.html.
33 See www.notimpossiblenow.com/lives/the-acclaimed-incubator-that-hospitals-never-used-and-what-designers-learned.
34 See www.reuters.com/article/us-health-newborns-kangaroo-care-idUSKBN0U522R20151222.
35 Radjou, N. & Prabhu, J. (2015). *Frugal Innovation: How to Do More with Less*. London: Profile Books.

2 Entrepreneurial strategy

Simon Mosey and Paul Kirkham

2.1 Introduction

In this chapter we consider what capabilities an organisation has for entrepreneurship and whether it should extend or change those capabilities. We use examples drawn from the car industry, Silicon Valley in California and local football clubs to help understand and explain different entrepreneurial options (in the following chapters we go on to explore how best these options can be deployed in more detail). We first suggest that traditional strategic planning, as taught in business schools for many years, is actually less useful when you are aiming to innovate and especially if you are seeking radical innovation because this approach places greater emphasis upon a more stable strategic environment.[1] Here an iterative approach to strategy – where organisations experiment within new areas and continually update their aims in the light of this new information – is more appropriate. We introduce three frameworks that explain the creation of new products, services, processes and business models more clearly and highlight how to use these to diagnose an organisation's current capabilities and prioritise future action.

We propose that there is no optimal strategic approach; rather, there are just different ways of considering and choosing entrepreneurial strategies. First, we introduce the idea of core competencies[2] as a set of skills and capabilities that an organisation uses to deliver distinctive and valuable products or services to existing customers; if your organisation is much better at doing that than your rivals, you are more likely to sustain a profitable position. If you are in the fortunate position of having such competencies, then future actions should focus upon nurturing and extending them. This is explained through the second framework of dynamic capabilities[3] that describes how to leverage existing competencies through developing new products and services, adopting new decision-making approaches and forming alliances with pioneering organisations. For the majority of organisations that don't have core competencies, we conclude with a framework called Blue Ocean Strategy[4]; this explains how to create new market value through radically disrupting existing business models.

2.2 The traditional view of strategy

The traditional view of strategy underpins the modern business school. A mainstay of this approach is the ubiquitous SWOT analysis. Meaning 'Strengths, Weaknesses, Opportunities and Threats', it suggests that as an organisation you look at internal strengths and weaknesses, you look at the external opportunities and threats facing you, you gather all the information together and then determine a course of action in the light of that analysis. It is an adversarial military-based model with large groups of analysts gathering information and then rationally planning what they need to do. This approach proved very successful for the corporate managers of global multinationals that dominated the world prior to the financial crisis that began in 2008. The landscape has changed, however, and it has changed quite drastically. Innovation is no longer dominated by a few multinationals, but instead smaller fast-moving organisations are emerging – organisations that have grown globally in a short space of time, and they are not working in this more traditional way. They work in very different ways.[5]

2.3 The entrepreneurial view of strategy

The traditional approach was created at a time when the external environment was changing in slow and predictable ways and the internal environment within an organisation was equally homogenous. However, we now face a very different reality where the external environment is complex and fast changing; consumer demands, political systems, the economic system and technological discontinuities are all changing at an ever-increasing rate.[6] As a result, it is much more difficult to plan for external change, especially long-term, but equally the internal dynamics of organisations are no longer as homogenous and predictable. People no longer join a big corporation, work for that corporation all their life and then retire. People are much more entrepreneurial with their careers; organisations are much more flexible and fast changing.

The following exchange helps to illustrate how the traditional model falls apart. In 1968 Paul Ehrlich wrote in *The Population Bomb*[7] 'The battle to feed all of humanity is over. In the 1970s the world will undergo famines – hundreds and millions of people are going to starve to death in spite of any crash-programmes embarked upon now'.

Ehrlich made this prediction based upon experts' views of the way crops were grown, the way resources were shared, and the way the population was growing around the world; he confidently predicted from that knowledge that millions were going to starve because there wouldn't be enough food and there would be war and famine.

A contemporary economist, Julian Simon,[8] disagreed with Ehrlich and made a wager that the price of key raw materials would fall rather than rise over the next ten years. Somewhat surprisingly, Simon won the bet. Ehrlich was allowed to select which were to be measured, so he chose copper, chrome, nickel, tin and tungsten, and over the specified ten-year period every one of those materials fell in price. Why was that? The fact remains that the world population increased with more and more people, with fewer and fewer resources, and yet those specified prices dropped. Simon explained that the surprising outcome was because more people with an increased income caused resources to become scarcer in the short term. However, scarcity causes prices to rise, higher prices present opportunities, and this prompts individuals and organisations to search for solutions. Many fail; many things are tried, and novel solutions are eventually found that could not be predicted based on historical data. New things that couldn't be visualised on the basis of conventional wisdom – new inventions, new ways of growing things, new seeds, new fertilizers, new ways of transporting things around, new ways of manufacturing, distributing and processing – were invented because of the high prices, and so the long-term prices fell. Predictions from the rational model were rapidly rendered obsolete by creative problem solving and invention in response to the opportunity created by rising prices.

Henry Mintzberg,[9] and more recently Eric Ries,[10] proposed that organisations should therefore abandon traditional approaches to strategy. They should still agree on an objective and specify a desire to innovate in a specific area, but rather than aiming to deliver against that plan they should try something out and experiment, evaluate the effects of that experiment and then – if they find something surprising, if something has changed in the meantime – adjust their objectives. Mintzberg called this *incrementalism*; Ries, the *lean approach*.

2.4 Entrepreneurial vs administrative approaches to strategy

Figure 2.1 helps to explain the prevalence of traditional versus entrepreneurial approaches, why organisations plan and work in different ways, and why some are much more supportive of entrepreneurship than others. According to Stevenson and Jarillo,[11] entrepreneurial management is characterised by the exploitation of opportunities, which is one end of a continuum as shown on the left in Figure 2.1. This is what they would call an entrepreneurial organisation, trying to find opportunities, pursuing those opportunities and then, if those opportunities aren't profitable, moving on to others. Such organisations experiment with a wide range of opportunities, try to grow rapidly and reward individuals based on creating new value. By contrast, on the right-hand side of the continuum is the administrative-focused organisation.

'Promoter' ←――――――――――――――――――――→ 'Trustee'

ENTREPRENEURIAL   ADMINISTRATIVE

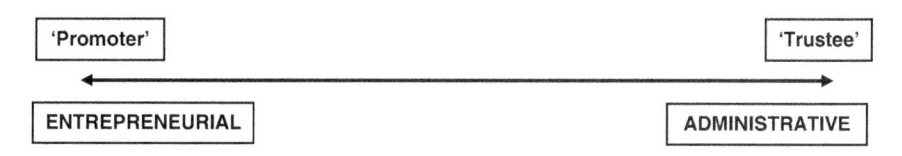

Figure 2.1 Adapted from Stevenson and Jarillo's continuum of entrepreneurial management.

Here the emphasis is upon controlling resources; you get promoted within this organisation not by creating new things but by managing a team efficiently and effectively, and the higher up in the organisation you go, the more people you have under your control. These organisations are typically very hierarchical, safe, slow and steady; you are not incentivised to search anywhere for opportunities. The only opportunities you are going to look for are ones that fit within your business remit. If something doesn't fit within what you are doing already, its gets rejected; if anyone pursues something that is not within the area of business it is seen as a failure and resources are removed (see Chapter 5 to see how to address these issues).

It is often revealing to consider your organisation and see where it fits along this continuum. You may be based in a small, fast-growing start-up thinking 'We need to be more organised, we need to manage resources better, we need more systems and procedures in place to control everything because it is just chaotic and it's all over the place' (see Chapter 7 for an exploration of this particular challenge). By contrast, you could be based in a large organisation thinking 'We used to be entrepreneurial, we are world leading now, we have got a surplus of cash but nobody within the organisation can come up with any new ideas because we have squeezed that out of the organisation due to the way we have managed things' (see Chapter 3 to explore how to overcome this barrier). In both cases new leaders may come in and try to move the organisation. If it's a large administrative organisation, these leaders act as a 'promoter' and try to make it more entrepreneurial pushing it to the left on the continuum. By contrast, if it's a small start-up doing all kinds of things, these leaders act as a 'trustee' and consequently try to focus on one thing and grow the organisation on the back of that focus. Organisations are constantly moving; at some point, probably in the middle of the continuum, you have got the perfect mix. You have an organisation that is managing its business as usual in an efficient and effective way but that is also looking for new opportunities. Unfortunately, organisations rarely stay in this 'bliss point' for any period of time. A consideration of the following analytical frameworks helps to explain why this is the case.

2.5 What are the core competencies of the organisation?

The first framework we recommend using to diagnose your organisation is the Core Competency model developed by Gary Hamel and C. K. Prahalad (1994; cited earlier). Their research followed organisations that seemed to be continually creating new forms of competitive advantage and they aimed to explain what these organisations were doing that was different. They concluded that these organisations had key skills, when compared with their rivals; Hamel and Prahalad called those key skills 'core competencies'. Such core competencies were found to be a complex bundle of skills and technologies rather than just a single discrete skill or technology. They highlighted exemplar organisations such as Federal Express which, they argued, has stayed number one in package delivery for so long because it has specific skill sets. These skills include integration of technology to scan and capture the data of customer parcels, together with the communications technologies to show where those parcels are in the world, the ability to manage that network, and the ability to programme the software in their systems to make sure that they move packages around and track them more efficiently than anyone else. Hamel and Prahalad proposed that core competencies were not dependent upon one charismatic leader or one superstar scientist; rather they are spread throughout the organisation. As a result organisations build-up such competencies over time, they are very difficult to copy and equally the organisation will be able to survive the departure of any one individual, no matter how influential that person may seem.

Hamel and Prahalad developed the following three tests to discern whether organisations have a core competence that will sustain their competitive position or whether their skill sets are not core and will therefore quickly erode.

2.5.1 Test 1: Delivering customer value

The first test for a core competence is whether the skill sets are able to deliver customer value. Here the idea is that the skills sets enable the organisation to deliver something to customers that they see as a fundamental benefit. A good example, and one of the reasons why it has been consistently rated the number-one company in terms of innovation, is Apple. According to its many customers around the world, Apple products and services are fundamentally better than their rivals, and customers therefore pay a premium price for them. The underlying skills that enable Apple to do this are a combination of their hardware-design capabilities and their proprietary software development. By closely integrating their award-winning product design with software that appears intuitive to the customer, they have consistently outperformed their rivals. Apple therefore has passed the first test by demonstrating a skill set that directly leads to customer value.

2.5.2 Test 2: Competitive differentiation

The second test is competitive differentiation; here, an organisation has a skill set that may not be exclusive to it, but its level of performance is superior to its rivals. Hamel and Prahalad illustrate this by using the example of Honda and the way it develops and builds engines more effectively than its rivals. Honda's advertising highlights how environmentally friendly and fuel efficient its engines are, and Honda is unusual in that it deploys its engines in cars, motorbikes, lawnmowers and even generators. Consider one of its rivals, such as Ford. Ford, of course, also makes engines; for the company, however, making engines is not core but is just necessary to compete within the car market. However, within this market Ford is competing on other factors rather than engine-development skills. Here, Honda outperform Ford in terms of engine development, a competence that is arguably better than that of Ford.

2.5.3 Test 3: Extendibility

The final test for core competence is the idea of extendibility. Hamel and Prahalad argue that a competence may offer value to current customers yet there needs to be a consideration of the future needs of customers. Organisations need to consider major trends and see how well positioned their competencies are to cover different possible future scenarios. Amazon is a good example to draw upon when considering extendibility. Amazon was one of the first online retailers and its mission from the start appeared to be the 'everything shop' – to be able to sell everything online. Amazon prospered through selling books and music but as new rivals appeared it realised that it had competencies that were valuable to other organisations as well as itself. This posed an interesting strategic decision. Amazon had to decide whether to keep the competencies to itself and outperform its rivals in the short term or sell its competencies as a service to rival firms and potentially retain a longer-term advantage. As a result, Amazon now offers its capabilities to other companies for one-click ordering, it offers access to its online marketplace to other sellers and it sells cloud software services. It appears to have concluded that it wants to retain the aim of being number one in online sales and distribution but it has also acknowledged that it is not quite sure how the future is going to unfold. The strategy ensures that, regardless of which service is number one, Amazon will still profit from its use of its proprietary recommendation engine, one-click ordering and cloud services. To paraphrase Mark Twain: in a gold rush, make sure you are selling picks and shovels. It doesn't matter who digs up the gold, if you are selling the picks and shovels you are going to make money. That is a very elegant example of making sure your competence is extendable to different future scenarios.

2.6 What a core competence is not

It is important to stress what a core competence is not because the field of competencies, capabilities and resources can be confusing.[12] By considering competencies, we are talking about skills – the ability to do things – rather than talking about the things themselves. A common misperception would be to consider an organisation such as Toyota and conclude that it has got an advantage because its factories are more efficient than those of other organisations and therefore its factories are a core competence. It is apparent that some of Toyota's factories are incredibly efficient, and Toyota pioneered methods of managing those factories such as just-in-time inventory and continuous improvement that others have since copied, but the factory itself is not a core competence. Toyota's ability to manage that factory could be a competence if it offers customer value and is differentiating and extendable, but the factory itself is not. This is equally true if you have a valuable brand like Coca-Cola; that brand is not a core competence but the ability to manage that brand and keep it number one could be a core competence. If the brand is the attribute that customers value, they will pay a premium for it, it is better than everyone else's and it is extendable. The point is that a brand or a factory can wear out over time and will erode but your capability to manage it, if you are better at doing it than anyone else, will sustain your competitive position.

2.7 Extending core competencies through to dynamic capabilities

Core competencies as a management framework became very popular yet inevitably it has its limitations. The central shortfall is that it is a hindsight measure. It is easy to analyse and explain core competencies for organisations that have been around for a long time, and you can look at what they have done and their performance and relate the two. Yet a core competence is very specific to individual organisations so it would be very difficult to say 'Right, we are going to start up a search engine organisation and we are going to build a core competence the same as Google's but better.' Even if you were managing Google and had performed the analysis you would still have to decide which of its original competencies you can leave and nurture and which new ones need to be developed. It seems that Google is experimenting with new competencies through its exploration of driverless cars and the Internet of Things. Yet future direction doesn't really come out of core competencies; you can't tell whether it's a core competence until after you have developed and deployed it, which is less useful in guiding future actions.

A new framework was therefore developed to help organisations extend their core competencies and stay ahead of the game, especially in the face of disruption. Teece *et al.*,[13] as well as Eisenhardt and Martin (2000; cited previously) looked within entrepreneurial organisations – organisations that have survived disruption and seem to prosper through disruption – and found that they engage in a series of activities which they called *dynamic capabilities*. These are similar to core competencies in that they are skills that are spread across the organisation and they are better at them than their rivals; however, they are not so path dependent and idiosyncratic and you don't have to examine a long period of time to isolate them. So for instance the ability to develop new products – if you are a service-based firm as demonstrated by Google with its driverless cars – is a dynamic capability. The ability to make entrepreneurial strategic decisions is another (see Pisano, 2015; we consider examples of this in the following chapter). The final dynamic capability is the ability to innovate in conjunction with other organisations; you are not just betting on the future yourself but you are working together with other groups. Within higher education, for example: in facing the challenge of online learning, many elite universities such as Harvard and MIT are collaborating to see what the value is in offering online learning; they are not necessarily going alone and doing their own thing (we will explore this activity in more detail in Chapter 6). So if you look within an organisation that is good at developing products, good at making strategic decisions and good at forming alliances and getting new knowledge into the organisation, you will find an organisation that is actually very good at extending its core competence. Yet many organisations are not in such a fortunate position and need to take a different approach as they find themselves without an obvious core competence to extend.

2.8 Doing things differently: Blue Ocean Strategy

The final strategy framework we would like to introduce was developed by Kim and Mauborgne (2005; cited earlier) and is most appropriate for those organisations that aim (or need) to do things differently. In their research, Kim and Mauborgne considered new business launches such as the creation of new ventures or the launch of new products or new services. Figure 2.2 shows that most new business launches are what we define as incremental innovations – slight improvements over what is already available. However, 14 per cent are what Kim and Mauborgne call *pioneering* and offer an innovation in customer value; we define these types of business launches as radical innovations as they provide new functionality and allow customers to do things that they couldn't do before. The reason why Kim and Mauborgne are interested in this smaller group of business launches arises from the very different financial implications of pioneering rather than incremental innovation-based businesses. Incremental, or 'me-too', business launches contribute 62 per cent to revenue and 39 per cent to profitability. By contrast the pioneering, radical launches contribute 38 per cent to revenue and a remarkable 61 per cent to profitability. So organisations that introduce radical innovations tend to be much more profitable than those that don't.

To illustrate this transition we are going to look within an industry that has really struggled with profitability and highlight an example of an organisation that's pioneering in terms of customer value. Kim and Mauborgne propose that

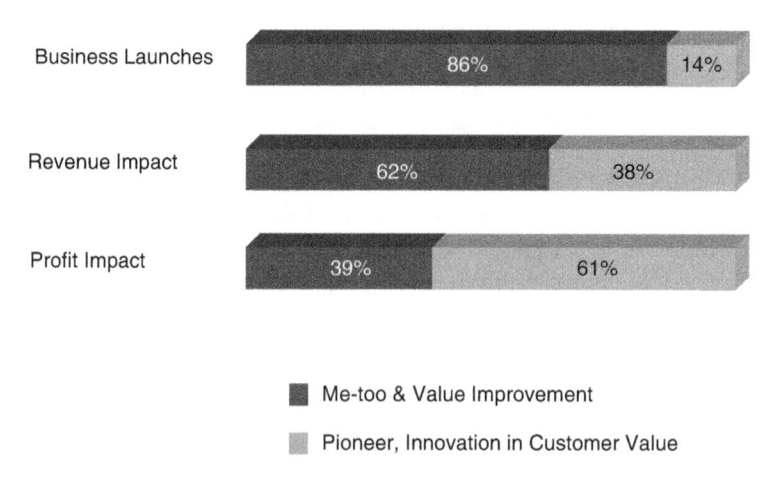

Figure 2.2 The financial implications of different types of innovations.
Source: adapted from Kim and Mauborgne (2005).

if your organisation is engaged in me-too value improvements you are competing in a red ocean, a bloodbath of organisations with similar competencies fighting over smaller and smaller market shares, thereby creating intense competition. By contrast, if you change your approach to create pioneering new customer value, then you can create a blue ocean where you are not competing with anyone.

2.9 Competing in a red ocean

An illustrative example of a red ocean is the global automotive industry. Table 2.1 shows profitability, return on sales for automotive industries around the world from 1970 to 2015.[14] Regardless of whether you consider the European car industry, the US or the Japanese, you will see a very low return on sales, sometimes negative. This suggests that this is an industry where there is very little innovation, many organisations are fighting over the same market, they are all doing similar things and incrementally changing what they are doing and relying predominantly upon large economies of scale. It is an extremely competitive industry and there is not a great deal of profitability.

2.10 A blue ocean example

Now against this red ocean backdrop, a radical new product was launched in 2008, the Tesla Roadster. This is a 100 per cent electric car that travels from 0 to 60 miles an hour in about 4 seconds. The Roadster is very fast, very stylish and very economical to run when compared to its rivals. Contemporary electric cars exhibit a perennial weakness in that they are perceived to be poor performing and don't travel very far between charges. When launched, the Roadster was celebrated as creating a blue ocean by attracting customers that wouldn't buy an existing electric car, and moreover attracting people that wouldn't buy any type of car (gas powered or electric) at all.[15]

2.11 Entrepreneurial practices to find a blue ocean

It is illustrative to examine the kind of organisation that developed this product and the entrepreneurial practices it used to find this blue ocean. Tesla Motors was actually founded by a group of Silicon Valley entrepreneurs including Martin Eberhard, Marc Tarpanning and Elon Musk. Elon Musk was the most well

Table 2.1 Percentage return on sales for the automotive industry

Year	1970	1975	1980	1985	1990	1995	2000	2005	2010	2015
European	3	2	2	2	3	0	3	1	−3	−1
Japanese	3	2	2	2	2	0	2	5	−3	0
US	3	1	2	−3	−4	3	8	1	−10	5

known, having been one of the founders of PayPal (which he exited to create Tesla), amongst other organisations. Notable investors included Sergey Brin and Larry Page of Google. Tesla was established in summer of 2003 and as of July 2009 it showed a positive return on sales.[16] For a start-up that is unusual; for the car industry it is quite remarkable. Tesla received a loan from the US government because of its environmentally friendly credentials. The company raised $265 million in an initial public offering, as it floated its shares on the US stock market; among its investors is a rival car company, Daimler Benz. Tesla has a radically different profile to the traditional large conglomerate that you would find within the car industry. In structure and organisation, it is more typical of a business in Silicon Valley, more like a creative start-up than a traditional manufacturing company. The entrepreneurial vision for the organisation is not as a car company but as a technology company. So although Tesla produces cars, what it sees itself producing is new technology: the battery pack, the software, the proprietary motor, that is, the power of the car. It is analogous to the Mark Twain picks and shovels dictum mentioned earlier. Tesla's vision of the future is the electric transmission of vehicles and it is delivering the underlying technology.[17]

To realise this vision Tesla has recruited executives and management ideas from the technology industry rather than just the car industry. The company gives stock options to every single employee, a practice from high-tech start-ups, and it does not supply its cars through independent dealers. Here Tesla has broken the traditional car supply chain to deal directly with the consumer. Considering the underlying technology, it was built from existing battery pack technology used in computers and the cell phone industry. A Tesla Roadster is powered by hundreds of bundles of lithium ion batteries and that allows it to outperform the battery pack seen in rival electric cars. Tesla has effectively imported an idea from a very different industry and brought it into the car industry to provide radically improved performance.

Building upon existing technology meant that Tesla was first to market, and at the outset the company protected its innovations with more than 20 patents around this technology. Despite its pioneering work, the company doesn't know what the future holds for electric cars, it doesn't know what the future holds for the car industry and more generally for electric vehicles. Consequently, it is pursuing an incrementalist strategy by growing the Tesla car range and concurrently licensing its power train and battery systems to Daimler, Toyota (Rav4) and Smart Cars. Tesla has created an open patent alliance to encourage rivals to adopt the technology and it is expanding battery production facilities in partnership with Panasonic.[18]

2.12 Paradigm change through doing without and doing differently

From the number of analytical tools presented by Kim and Mauborgne the eliminate-reduce-raise-create (ERRC) actions framework is particularly useful in that it provides guidelines to identify new competing factors. Table 2.2 uses

Table 2.2 ERRC framework showing the paradigm change for Tesla Roadster

Raise	*Reduce*
Electric car acceleration	Electric car running costs
Electric car range	Range of models
Create	*Eliminate*
Stylish electric car	Use of independent dealers
Home battery-charging system	Servicing

Source: adapted from Baer (2014), Girotra and Netessine (2013) and Musk (2006).

this framework to show how Tesla changed the paradigm of the car industry with the Tesla Roadster. Here we see four categories of possible changes. The first, in the lower left, shows changes that are traditionally associated with innovation, the creation of new things. Tesla has clearly created a beautiful and stylish electric car that is fun to drive and it has created a built-in battery-charging system that is compatible with outlets in the home. The top left quadrant shows the features Tesla has raised relative to their rivals. It has raised the energy efficiency compared to hybrid and electric vehicles and other cars; it has raised the driving range and the acceleration rate. These are the most obvious changes; the features Tesla has added. Traditional car companies have competencies in these areas and therefore could, in theory, extend their competencies to create more stylish and more efficient electric vehicles. However, on the right-hand side of the table are the changes that have arguably been responsible for the durability of Tesla's blue ocean advantage. Here we see that Tesla, unencumbered by competencies from the car industry, has been able to eliminate and reduce key aspects associated with the existing car paradigm. Tesla was therefore able to reduce elements it never relied upon such as having to offer a full range of car models. Moreover, it was able to eliminate significant aspects of the car paradigm such as complex maintenance. The Roadster has no motor oil, no oil filters, no air filters and no power steering fluid; as a consequence, the whole service schedule of the car has been transformed through the introduction of the new battery and the power train. It is a much cleaner and completely different business model compared to the traditional automotive industry, especially through the removal of the role of independent dealerships. Table 2.2 captures graphically this disruption; where it is most evident both for consumers and competitors is where they have 'done without' through elimination.

2.13 Conclusion: Entrepreneurial strategy in practice

This chapter has offered frameworks to diagnose the strategic position of an organisation and determine the strategic options in light of that diagnosis. Yet the examples cited are all with the benefit of hindsight. It is therefore instructive to address a contemporary example to highlight the utility of the presented frameworks. Readers are encouraged to use the core competence, dynamic capabilities and ERRC framework to diagnose the strategic situation and propose an entrepreneurial strategy for Case 2.1.

CASE 2.1 FOOTBALL CRAZY

According to FIFA (Fédération Internationale de Football Association), the 2014 World Cup Final was seen by more than one billion people worldwide.[19] The TV signal was received by 214 countries, FIFA's social media content reached 451 million Facebook users and a total of 3,240 footballs were used for the whole tournament. Football is arguably the most popular sport in history and at the higher levels it is certainly one of the richest. According to the BBC rights for live TV coverage of three seasons of the English Premier League from 2016–17 to 2018–19 were sold for £5.136 billion.[20] Despite the fact that most professional football clubs seem to be run for the benefit of their workforce rather than their owners, there is no shortage of entrepreneurs and business people willing to involve themselves in football. It may be a beautiful game in theory but it is a far from beautiful business in practice – something that appears to be true at all levels of the game. In the example that follows, put yourself in the position of chairman of an English football club of somewhat modest circumstances.

The Club

Anytown Wanderers AFC plays in the Northern League, level 9 of the Football Association (FA). At different times since their founding in 1889 the club has been both professional and semi-professional, but since 1937 it has enjoyed amateur status.

The stadium capacity is 1,500 and is rarely filled. In the event of a decent draw in the cup there is ample car parking on the adjoining training pitch.

The club is not without enterprise: last year they hosted a successful two-day music festival in the summer and a fireworks display in November. Both were well attended and profitable enough to be repeated this year.

The social club, too, is thriving and offers facilities for weddings and other functions.

The club maintains a lively online presence with match reports, photos and videos available on their own site, YouTube, Instagram and other social media sites.

Despite its present lowly standing the club has had its moments. It won the FA Amateur Cup five times, first in 1901 and most recently in 1964. By the 1920s they had toured Spain on three occasions, playing the mighty

Barcelona a total of ten times (with a record of Won 2 Lost 4 Drawn 4). One member of the squad stayed on, playing for and managing Barcelona before coaching the national team in the 1930s. In 1976 they were the first English club side to tour India; they played six matches, including a one–nil defeat to the Indian national team in front of 100,000 spectators.

However, all that was some time ago; apart from a few brief revivals the club is languishing. Most people agree that the club could not survive without the advice and encouragement of the club's president, local businessman Ben E. Factor. He has given freely of his time and considerable business acumen and he has provided much needed income through his organisation's advertising and sponsorship.

The challenge

For the purposes of this exercise it is assumed that the club is ambitious: players, coaches, staff and fans are all on board and are eager to move up to the next level. There are a couple of hurdles to overcome, however.

As you may know, the FA has strict rules. In the lower echelons it is not uncommon for teams to forego promotion because their ground does not meet FA standards. Even if Anytown Wanderers were to win the league, the ground would need an urgent upgrade.

More urgently, Mr. Factor has announced that he will be selling his business interests and moving abroad to a well-earned retirement in the south of France. He has generously given the club notice that he will cease his involvement in two years.

What next?

Establish whether the club has a core competence by asking the following questions:

1. Do the Anytown Wanderers have a combination of skills and technologies that offer customer value?
2. Do they have a combination of skills and technologies that are competitively distinct?
3. Do they have a combination of skills and technologies that are extendable?

If a core competence is identified, recommend which dynamic capabilities should be developed to extend the competence (new product or service development, entrepreneurial decision making, entrepreneurial alliances).

If a core competence cannot be identified, then establish whether a blue ocean strategy can be created by asking the following question:

4. What can they raise, create, reduce or eliminate to do things differently or do without?

For a summary of some of the observations that this case has provided in the past, please see section 2.15. But to understand the benefits that can arise from these ideas, please ensure that you undertake the exercise before considering how others have responded.

2.15 Example case responses

1. Wimbledon FC rose from English non-league obscurity in the last quarter of the 20th century. Rapid promotion to the top flight and an FA Cup win in 1988 over the league champions Liverpool demonstrate the core competence of a high growth business. But how can you extend that competence when you cannot develop your stadium and are forced to share with your rivals? How can you build a substantial following in the competitive environment of London football with its long list of famous names? The answer, unprecedented in English football, was through an unusual alliance and subsequent new service offer. The team chose to relocate some 56 miles north of Wimbledon, specifically to Milton Keynes, a 'new town' with no long established competition. After several ups and downs the new club – MK Dons – is now happily ensconced in the second tier of English football.

2. What if you have no core competence that you can develop to distinguish yourself from the competition? How much can you realistically charge the sponsor for the kit of a club in the third division of the Brazilian league where shirt sales amount to around ten per month? The answer for Madureira Esporte Clube came when, following a tour of Cuba, they took the blue ocean approach of doing without a club sponsor for their shirts. They substituted a sponsor with the iconic face of Che Guevara on their kit; worldwide sales rocketed and the new challenge is to keep up with demand.

References

1 Pisano, G. (2015). 'You need an innovation strategy', *Harvard Business Review*. June: 44–54.
2 Hamel, G. & Prahalad, C.K. (1994). *Competing for the Future*. Cambridge, Mass.: Harvard Business School Press.
3 Eisenhardt, K.M. & Martin, J.A. (2000). 'Dynamic capabilities, what are they?', *Strategic Management Journal*, 21: 1105–1121.
4 Kim, W.C. & Mauborgne, R. (2005). *Blue Ocean Strategy: How to Create Uncontested Market Space and Make the Competition Irrelevant*. Cambridge, Mass.: Harvard Business School Press.
5 Martin, R. (2013). 'The future of business and the role of business education'. Paper presented at the Academy of Management Conference, Orlando, Florida.
6 D'Aveni, R.A., Dagnino, G.B. & Smith, K.G. (2010). 'The age of temporary advantage', *Strategic Management Journal*, 31(13): 1371–1385.
7 Ehrlich, P. (1968). *The Population Bomb*. New York: Ballantine Books.
8 Simon, J. (1996). *The State of Humanity*. New York: Blackwell.
9 Mintzberg, H. (2004). *Managers not MBAs: A Hard Look at the Soft Practice of Managing and Management Development*. San Francisco: Berrett-Koehler Publishers.

10 Ries, E. (2011). *The lean Startup: How constant Innovation Creates Radically Successful Businesses.* New York: Portfolio Penguin.
11 Stevenson, H. & Jarillo, J.C. (1990). 'A paradigm of entrepreneurship: Entrepreneurial management', *Strategic Management Journal*, 11: 17–27.
12 Sirmon, D.G., Hitt, M.A., Arregle, J.-L. & Campbell, J.T. (2010). 'The dynamic interplay of capability strengths and weaknesses: Investigating the bases of temporary competitive advantage', *Strategic Management Journal*, 31(13): 1386–1409.
13 Teece, D.J., Pisano, G. & Shuen, A. (1997). 'Dynamic capabilities and strategic management', *Strategic Management Journal*, 18(7): 509–533.
14 See http://topforeignstocks.com/2010/11/29/why-investing-in-auto-stocks-is-complex/; http://financials.morningstar.com/ratios/r.html?t=TSLA.
15 Baer, D. (2014). 'The making of Tesla: Invention, betrayal, and the birth of the Roadster', *Business Insider*, November 11.
16 Girotra, K. & Netessine, S. (2013). 'At last, a new business model for Tesla', *Harvard Business Review*, July 2013.
17 Musk, E. (2006). 'The secret Tesla Motors master plan (just between you and me)'. See www.tesla.com/fr_CH/blog/secret-tesla-motors-master-plan-just-between-you-and-me.
18 Porter, M. & Heppelmann, J. (2014). 'How smart, connected products are transforming competition', *Harvard Business Review*, July 14.
19 See www.fifa.com/worldcup/news/y=2015/m=12/news=2014-fifa-world-cuptm-reached-3-2-billion-viewers-one-billion-watched–2745519.html.
20 See www.bbc.co.uk/sport/football/31357409.

3 Strategy in practice

Insights from an entrepreneurial multinational

Jim Crilly and Paul Kirkham

3.1 Introduction

This chapter considers how to deploy an entrepreneurial strategy within arguably the most challenging context of a multinational organisation. We draw from a series of interviews with Jim Crilly, Senior Vice President for Research at Unilever. We share his experience of how to create and sustain an entrepreneurial strategy, based upon his 30 years' experience of entrepreneurship within food, home and personal care products that currently generate billions of pounds in global sales. We explain a simplified framework for the strategy-development process, highlighting the key inputs and considerations required and how the process needs to be iterative and inclusive, top down and bottom up. Some specific examples of successful innovations are highlighted to illustrate how Unilever mobilised its core competencies in deep consumer insight fused with timely new technology development. We share how Unilever extended its competencies through alliances, product development and entrepreneurial decision making to achieve sales growth whilst reducing environmental impact. We conclude that strategy development is fractal[1] in nature and consequently, the approaches highlighted from Unilever can be adopted by any size of organisation.

3.2 The need for an entrepreneurial strategy at Unilever

At Unilever in the early 1980s, there had been a far-reaching strategic realignment – major disposals followed by major acquisitions. At that time, Unilever was a much more diversified company in terms of business portfolio than in its present form. Its business interests were very broad and included plastics, packaging, tropical plantations and even a shipping line alongside core product categories in foods, home and personal care. It was also vertically integrated in areas such as foods with major agricultural operations in farming and fishing. The company decided to refocus on core consumer product areas with strong markets and equally strong growth potential. Consequently, in the years after 1984, categories such as animal feeds, packaging, transport and fish farming were sold and the emphasis for growth was placed upon consumer products.

Since then, the leadership team has conducted a series of major strategy developments including a review of innovation and technology in the early 1990s and then, over the following 20 years, a number of strategic reviews and planning initiatives, including the Foods Research and Development (R&D) strategy conducted from 1998 to 2000, the Ice Cream category strategy considered between 2006 and 2008 and finally, the (functional) R&D strategy.

Over this extended period Unilever sought the advice of expert consultants on strategy such as those at HAX, Boston Consulting Group, Value Engineers and Viadynamics. Jim's view was that some of these approaches were very analytical and quantitative with deep dives and forward planning, whereas others were much more vision-oriented and projective onto an ideal future state/performance of the company. Nonetheless, all these approaches were concluded to be valid and demonstrated utility depending on the task at hand, as we shall see in the following sections.

3.3 Unilever's definition of an entrepreneurial strategy

A key finding from these strategic reviews was the need for clarity and consistency in the language used regarding strategy across the organisation. As Jim argues:

> I think there is confusion in the language people use. People talk about vision and values - mission statements and so on – they use the word 'strategic' to mean big or important - you know the sort of thing 'I'm strategic – you are operational'. But it is a lot more than that. It comes from the Greek στρατηγία and it's an art of leadership. It is how you deploy your resources to achieve your objectives.

As a result, Unilever's leadership team tried to make everyone understand their views of strategy by sharing the following common definition across the organisation:

- Mission is 'why we exist'.
- Values are 'what's important to us'.
- Vision is 'where we want to be'.
- Strategy is 'how we are going to get there'.
- It's all about envisioning the future.

After agreeing upon common terms, the discussion progressed towards the timescales over which they would focus. They concluded that an effective strategy should embrace short-, medium- and long-term objectives. For example, considering Jim's area of responsibility – driving growth through R&D – they developed different language for the different timescales. In the short term the key word was 'manage'; the aim was to defend, support and expand the current business through unlocking incremental growth but managing for value as that business declines.

By contrast, the medium term focused upon nurturing emerging business and developing new brands; the key word here was 'build'. And for the long term the key word was 'explore', through sourcing and creating viable new options across multiple scenarios. These different perspectives were observed to create tension between different parts of the business and it became clear that a short-term focus had historically dominated the decision making. As a result it was concluded that the organisation needed to inculcate a longer term view, but to do so necessitated a very different approach, as Jim explained:

> Short of having extraordinary psychic powers, it is not possible to predict the future exactly. Now if the future were to be just an extrapolation of the past through the present, shaped by the major global trends affecting a business enterprise, then predicting the future world would be much more straightforward. However, it isn't quite like that – 'stuff happens' – perturbing events and discontinuities. There is more than one future, in fact multiple futures, and that's why business leaders and strategic planners think in terms of the most likely scenarios. And don't forget the pace of change is accelerating – we are living in a volatile, uncertain, complex and ambiguous world which makes simple forecasting ineffectual. So, in addition to a compelling vision, the best approach for any enterprise seeking a long-term future should be to develop a responsiveness and agility to cope with the vicissitudes that will come.

3.4 Codifying Unilever's entrepreneurial strategy

Given the leadership's recognition of the need for responsiveness and agility, they committed significant resources to developing a new mission, vision and blueprint for success. In consultation with key stakeholders across the organisation and at all levels, they developed the following statements to codify and share their new entrepreneurial strategy:

- Our mission (why we exist): *Make Sustainable Living Commonplace.*
- The vision: *Double the size of the business, whilst reducing our environmental footprint and increasing our positive social impact.*
- The blueprint for success: *Identify what we must do to win share and grow volume in every category and country.*

When they developed this strategy it became apparent that alignment was very important so they agreed on the need for these messages to be shared and understood throughout the company. They talked about creativity being scalable, to be expected throughout the company, and leadership being modelled at all levels against the background of a shared understanding of where they were going. These principles were captured within an internal document called 'The Compass', a document that more fully articulated the company's aim to achieve significant growth whilst minimising its impact on the environment.[2]

However, despite the significant consultative and inclusive effort incurred in developing and sharing this document, Jim argued that it was found to be just the beginning of a significant journey of strategy deployment:

> This is where the hard work begins. The Compass isn't a map, it's a direction. The strategy is all about how to proceed in that direction. It's based on business need – what the business wants to achieve against the various competitive aspects of its industrial landscape. What their current commitments are, what consumers want to do – it's challenging. Strategy development itself is not a straightforward process. You don't do it in a week or a month, it very often takes several years to really forge what it is you have to do. It's worth the investment because you may be driving a growth strategy for five, ten or more years.

To highlight the complexity of the task at hand, underpinning the strategy was a common understanding that, for businesses in Unilever's sector, the key requirements were consumer insight and speed to market. Consumer insight was acknowledged to provide a competitive edge, but despite the company's prestigious customer-data sources, the leadership reflected on how often they were complacent regarding exactly which consumer need they were meeting. In a similar vein, when considering speed to market they reflected that although they had an advantage over their rivals, any advantage was soon eroded by imitation. They also reflected that innovation within fast-moving consumer goods (FMCG) in particular has to be considered much more broadly than just the products. For instance, following the observation that mainstream-media advertising was fading as a source of competitive advantage, an increased emphasis had to be placed upon social media and other online sources, necessitating a new conceptualisation of the complete integrated life of the consumer. In sum, Unilever needed to consider innovation of technology, channels, manufacturing, outlets, innovation in brands and marketing; it was all a complex landscape that was changing constantly.

3.5 The entrepreneurial strategy development process

When attempting to deploy its strategic document, Unilever found that strategy-development processes are by necessity nested in character; they often use the word 'fractal'. That is, the corporate strategy is on the outer or higher fractal plane; the business, category, regional and finally pillar (functional) strategies are in the lower planes. Leadership found that there were many more inputs and considerations to be taken at the pillar level. Although it all stemmed from the corporate vision and strategy cascading down to the category and functional strategies, they found that the processes were highly iterative; top down then bottom up. They found the recycling back and forth to be essential in gaining the alignment and coherence between the vision and the enterprise objectives and the comprehensive plan to deploy the resources on the key priorities. Despite the complexity of the organisation in terms of different functions, levels and geographic location, they were surprised to discover the fractal nature of the process, that the same broad inputs applied right across the company, at all levels. These were codified within the following three steps of reviewing, scanning and optioning:

3.5.1 Reviewing

Reviewing entailed each function considering the following questions: Where do we stand – what can we do? What do we currently have in terms of current commitments, what's coming through the pipeline, what have we got in terms of brand equities? What are our core competencies? What technological capabilities do we have? What opportunities are presented by new technologies that are largely going in the direction we want to go and what technical hurdles do we have to overcome to go in a certain direction to fulfil our vision?

3.5.2 Scanning

Scanning required that each function ask the following questions: What's going on out there? What are the current trends? Where are consumers moving, where is the brand moving, where is the world moving, where is regulation moving? What are the technology trends? What are our competitors' trends? Can we 'war game' our rivals? What are the consumer concerns? What are trends towards health, convenience, personalisation and experience consumption? What are consumers' wider concerns surrounding ethics and sustainability? These factors came to be codified within the following saying that was shared across the organisation: 'We are replacing selling brands to consumers with mattering to people'.

3.5.3 Optioning

Optioning required considering the What if …? questions. For instance, what if someone (internally or externally) comes up with an entirely new proposition – like bagged lettuce (see Chapter 5). On the other hand, what if a major acquisition target becomes available? What about external disruptions? For instance, how many companies had factored in the possibility of a crisis in the Ukraine in 2014?

By comparing how these three steps were deployed across different functions, Jim observed that the general template and vision remained consistent. For instance, when considering a single product from Unilever's portfolio, through using this approach the company should be able to forecast the business fade, the drop in contribution to overall profit over time. Leadership would know there was a balance to be struck on pricing, as when a particular product was new to market they would be able set the price high because the value was embedded in the new benefits it was bringing and consumers evaluated that against the price being charged. When the company reached a critical mass of sales, profitability would increase and it could then afford to drop the price. However, that balance would inevitably be upset by the reaction of the competition. Here leadership would have to consider how best to protect the product from imitation. This is where the underlying technology could provide an advantage. Yet just as products can be imitated, the same could be seen for technologies. In the embryonic stage, technology would develop in parallel with the new product. In the growth stage it would have the maximum impact and then inevitably it will hit maturity and become obsolete. It may still have value but it would not offer the same competitive advantage they had before. Consequently, the short-term options for management of the product innovation could be line extensions or it could be an exit. By contrast, over the medium term it would be more appropriate to explore new outlets such as through brand development. Finally, over the long term, leadership would need to explore radical technological changes, hopefully leading to a significant cost advantage. In sum, they ought to be able to predict the gap that they will have to fill with innovation in order to combat business fade. They developed the new practices of envisaging 'future snapshots' and creating milestones to mark their progress towards them. This represents consistent and sustained effort to change practices, as Jim summarises:

> The thing to dispel is that somehow strategy development is just an inspiration – 'Oh yeah I have got it!' Quite the opposite – it's a consequence of a lot of work done in a very structured and integrated way. Visions often don't come about that way either, as a matter of fact – they are the consequence of hard work also. It's important to dispel the myth of people one day saying 'I had a big idea that this was going to happen and I knew immediately how to do it' – it usually doesn't work that way.

3.6 Identifying Unilever's core competencies in research and development

It is instructive to consider how strategy development was conducted within R&D, Jim's area of responsibility, in more detail. Here the focus was in technology. When Unilever created new products it often needed new technology to enable new ways of doing things. Yet, the company found that the advantage of new technology was eroding more quickly over time and as a consequence it needed an increasing emphasis upon a portfolio of technologies, each having different impacts: from emerging technologies that were not well understood to those that were used by everyone.

These new technologies could be manifest in different ways. It might be a new technology of manufacturing, or the technology associated with supply chain in terms of ingredients or materials. Maybe the new product would be a different technology or a disruptive technology. Leadership agreed that a key technology is the one everybody wants to have, it is something that can be well embedded in products, in packaging, in the manufacturing or in the supply chain, and it will have high competitive impact. But they agreed that even if the company has technology with patents that last 20 years, these patents will lapse,[3] with the consequence that the market is open for all their competitors to come in and copy. As a result, they would also rely on things like trade secrets, the knowledge that's embedded in their employees.

Periodically, new technology would originate from the creation of new knowledge arising from the science base, and this will create new unforeseen possibilities. So science becomes technology, technology can underpin radical innovation and such innovation can exponentially grow the business. However, the R&D team at Unilever were at pains to differentiate scientific efforts from technology development, as Akio Morita, the former head of Sony, famously cited: 'Don't mistake science for technology or technology for innovation: they are not the same thing'.[4]

The R&D team realised that science may incorporate new knowledge, but that doesn't mean it *does* anything for the consumer in the market place until it was translated into a useable technology that can then underpin the benefits of a product. This is the development pathway that takes place with new technology, yet it can be discontinuous and unpredictable. Jim reflected upon the story of 3M and the Post-it note (see Chapter 9) and noted that the technology was discovered in 1968 but didn't get to market until 1981. That's how long it took to get an alignment inside the company to bring it along, to find the real consumer value in it and to find a business outlet for it. On the other hand, another well-known example of the impact of technological change was realised within Kodak over a much shorter timeframe. Jim reflected that Kodak was overtaken in the market by digital photography – a technology Kodak was instrumental in developing. Kodak's view was that this was a technological innovation that would appeal to specialists. What the company missed was the mass-market opportunity for a fast-snaps process by the consumer at home. The lesson Jim took from this was that Unilever shouldn't be complacent about what customers really want. A prime example can be seen in how the company needed to be vigilant about converging technologies – the Internet of Things – and how that is changing and disrupting consumer perceptions and behaviours. Jim summarises the importance of managing this delicate balance between short-term technology development and longer-term technology threats as:

> In some ways strategy development is a nice dreaming process which you can go through creating your vision and looking at how you do it. Strategy deployment is where you really put your money on the table and you make things happen. Yes, you might have the big idea, but making it happen is a different ball game; more straight-forward in many ways but tough because it involves people, it involves big decisions, it involves big investments. When you've a budget of €1 billion and 6,000 people's jobs at stake, it concentrates the mind.

3.7 Extending Unilever's R&D core competencies through product development

Following the strategy-development process within the Unilever R&D team, they concluded that they had core competencies in consumer insight yet they needed to extend their R&D competencies to meet the blueprint for success of: *identify what we must do to win share and grow volume in every category and country*.

Considering the specific product category of ice cream highlights how Unilever achieved this goal by extending their R&D competency through radical new ice cream product development. Within ice cream, Unilever concentrates on strong brands with strong technologies and protects them through legal agreements, copyrights, patents and trade secrets. And when everything is put together the company finds itself with a proposition that's very hard to imitate. Unilever divides the ice cream market into the following four sectors:

1. Impulse – trade cabinets in shops or stalls – bought for immediate consumption.
2. Multipacks – the same range as impulse but sold in supermarkets for consumption in the home.
3. Portion at point of sale – scoops, soft ices, slush – freshly prepared for the consumer; any flavour, any topping for immediate consumption.
4. Home vending – the same range as seen for sector 3, but from a large tub, bought in the supermarket and dispensed from the consumer's freezer at home.

Unilever has a significant data advantage over its rivals in that it knows the trends in each sector, in every town in every part of the world that it is selling into – those that are increasing, those that are declining, where the growth potential is, what the technologies are, which are the strongest brands.

This knowledge was famously deployed within the Magnum product, a new category of premium chocolate-coated ice cream products, which came out of an awareness of the market, an understanding of its customers, a recognition of a trend towards indulgence and the capability of developing a technology to defend a new product. This provided a perfect combination of a focus on consumers through recognising an opportunity to develop a strong brand with a strong technology.

The challenge which Jim faced in leading the ice cream research team was how to achieve sustainable growth in this area. The first step was to consider line extensions; they subsequently developed a range of Magnum variants including Magnum Double and Magnum Caramel, and limited-edition ranges such as Magnum Seven Deadly Sins and Magnum Five Senses. Each offered different levels of sensory pleasure through different flavours of ice cream and variations of chocolate coating.

The innovation challenge posed to the brand team and to R&D was to take a big step further and create a new product platform which could bring the full sensorial impact of a dessert ice cream with high levels of inclusions and sauces, all encapsulated in a chocolate-coated impulse product on a stick. A detailed survey of existing technologies from strategic suppliers showed that none could meet these requirements. The R&D team had been working on two major processing technology platforms which in combination was proven to be able to deliver such a product. These were proprietary technologies and the team was careful to build an intellectual property rights (IPR) portfolio to ensure that the barrier to competitor imitation would be high. Making the product uniquely dependent on the *fusion* of two proprietary technologies provided additional hurdles to imitation. The R&D team also developed innovative packaging which added to both the uniqueness and superior quality of the breakthrough product which was launched as Magnum Temptation to record sales. Jim and the research team were justifiably proud of the outcome, as he stated:

> It was just so satisfying to eventually reach the market with this breakthrough technology delivering a product matched to an emerging consumer need but with a high competitive barrier. It was one – and a rare one – of those innovations which brought all the pieces together to make a winner!

3.8 Extending Unilever's R&D core competencies through alliances

In 1989 Unilever acquired Elizabeth Arden, a US-based cosmetics company which provided the opportunity for Unilever to extend its multinational research capabilities into the high-end cosmetics market. Elizabeth Arden's customers had provided feedback stating that one of the lipsticks was rather waxy, it came off too easily and it dried the lips. As a result, the Unilever R&D team explored whether they had any knowledge that they could use to address this challenge. They were able to help and the eventual product launched was Lip Spa – a moisturising lipstick that went on to become a very successful global brand. What was remarkable was the knowledge that Unilever R&D deployed came from their food division. As Jim explains:

> We think we recognise that problem because our original margarines were high in fat – it was pretty thick. And so the water-structuring technology we used to develop low fat spreads like Flora was the start of a potential solution. Obviously we needed to do a lot of work adding different types of waxes to give it strength and of course pigments for colour, but you could say that basically we took the structure of a spread and put in a lipstick!

This case provides a valuable illustration of the principal of recombinant innovation,[5] taking a solution from one product category and applying it to another. Between 1990 and 2010, Unilever R&D extended their capabilities repeatedly through this process, most famously when they invented and launched the world's leading pregnancy test product ClearBlue™, which came out of work from an unrelated team in health immunology.

3.9 Extending Unilever's R&D core competencies through entrepreneurial decision making

Building upon the success of product development and innovating through alliances, the R&D team also experimented with their decision-making processes. Here the teams that were formed temporarily across categories and disparate geographic locations came together to informally subvert the usual product development decision-making process to develop Dove 'Strength Within' – a breakthrough in controlling skin wrinkles through gene signalling. It provided a disruptive proposition within the cosmetics market as it was eventually delivered in the form of a capsule and provided benefits that were clinically proven. The development team realised early in the development process that their conventional mass-market retail selling wasn't going to work with such a product; beauty salons were a more appropriate and possibly the perfect outlet. If the R&D team had presented this concept to the traditional decision-making team, it would have been rejected as not within scope of the existing business model. Yet the team persisted through mobilising an informal network of people who had known each other a long time and were able to bridge the organisational and functional divides to get the product to market. Jim summarises the value of this approach:

> This example corroborates the findings reported by others that informal networks really do make big innovations happen. You need the formal process but also an informal structure. So much of the talk around innovation is really common sense but it's very easy to forget the basics. I call them platitudes because they state the obvious but you'd be surprised how often we need to repeat them:
> 1 Strategy has no effect until it is deployed.
> 2 Technology gives no competitive advantage until it is used.
> 3 People are not an asset until you let them contribute.
> 4 Winners are usually characterised by the will to win.

3.10 Conclusion: A scalable approach to strategy

Our consideration of strategy development at Unilever emphasises the sustained and comprehensive effort required to share a new entrepreneurial vision of growth through sustainability and social responsibility. We described how different innovation challenges were generated and, through addressing these challenges, how the core competencies of the organisation were extended and enhanced. We suggested that these practices were highly dependent upon the knowledge and networks of people across the organisation and their inclusion to help develop the strategy and then deliver against the vision. And critically, we contend that such practices are more generally applicable than the context of Unilever, as Jim's concludes:

> And the thing I really want to get across is that all these factors – creativity, participative management, strategy development – are scalable; you don't have to be a multinational, you can build them in at all levels in any size of organisation.

We now consider, in Chapter 4, the need to build a supportive culture to allow such practices to flourish.

References

1 'Fractal' is a mathematical term, extended here into an organisational setting to highlight a pattern that is exactly repeated at a smaller scale.
2 See www.unilever.co.uk/aboutus/ourhistory/2000s/index.aspx.
3 Within most geographic regions, patent protection is granted for 20 years only.
4 Morita, A. (1992). '*S*' *does not equal 'T' and 'T' does not equal 'I'*. London: The First United Kingdom Innovation Lecture.
5 Hargadon, A. (2003). *How Breakthroughs Happen: The Surprising Truth About How Companies Innovate*. Cambridge, Mass.: Harvard Business School Press.

4 Entrepreneurial culture and leadership

Structure, processes and people

Hannah Noke and Simon Mosey

4.1 Introduction

Within this chapter we explore how organisations can build a culture of entrepreneurship to deliver innovative outcomes. Despite the best intentions of leaders and managers in developing an entrepreneurial strategy, this will be unlikely to lead to success if the organisation is bureaucratic, stifles creativity and places a stranglehold on autonomy. Figure 4.1 highlights the different elements that are necessary, but not sufficient on their own, to sustain such an entrepreneurial culture. This chapter will consider in turn these elements of organisational structure, entrepreneurial processes, people and leadership, and it will then explore how they interact. In this way a framework is developed for diagnosing the entrepreneurial culture within any organisation.

4.2 Organisational structure for entrepreneurship

As an organisation grows, its structure will naturally evolve and change. This can be conceptualised as an organisational life cycle.[1] At the beginning of an organisation's life it is likely to be informal in nature and entrepreneurial, with little need for real structure or formalisation. This is often because the organisation centres around the lead entrepreneur/s and it is at this stage that the entrepreneur or those within the founding team are working to ensure the survival of the organisation (see Churchill & Lewis[2]). Through managing all the different functions of the business from finance, marketing, sales to operations, at the beginning the founders are the core of the organisation. As the organisation grows and employs more people, there is a need for more formalisation to be introduced in the way of processes and procedures, supported by a more functional approach to the organisation. Departmental functions begin to emerge to support the growing number of people and meet the increasing demand from expanding products and/or services. As growth continues, organisations can choose to adopt a decentralised structure or organise themselves geographically around profit centres. This enables specialism and eventually core competencies to be built.

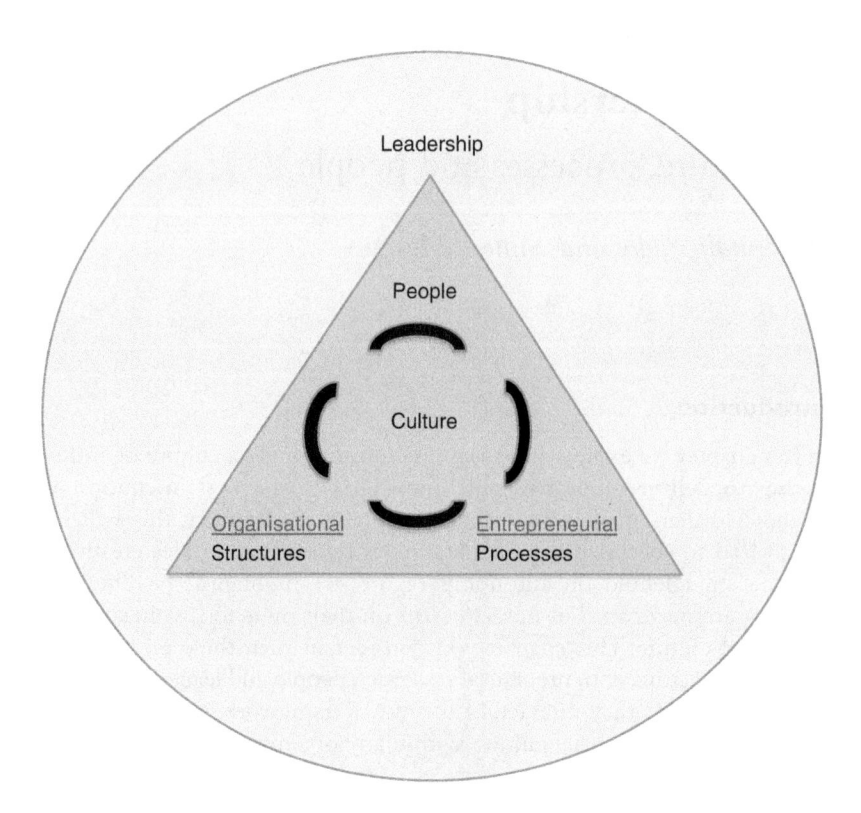

Figure 4.1 The elements of culture within an entrepreneurial organisation.

Whichever way the organisation approaches its growth, the structure will have to change; there is no one best way in which to structure an organisation, however. This is very much dependent on the nature of the organisation and the industry within which it operates. Mintzberg identified several organisational configurations or archetypes operating successfully in very different environments.[3] The structure of an organisation can therefore be more usefully viewed as structural transition; continually adjusting to external pressures and internal priorities. The key issue to note here is that entrepreneurship and innovation are often undermined in the course of restructuring efforts. The desire to manage the organisation often dominates and overrides the need for entrepreneurship, with innovation being relegated to the sidelines as financial control and a need to meet stakeholder demands take centre stage.

For innovation to be sustained, the organisational structure needs to enable creative thinking, collaboration, empowerment, room to manoeuvre, flexibility in resources and time available, good communication and tolerance of failure. Burns and Stalker[4] identified an organic structure to be the most supportive of innovation, regardless of whether the organisation is divided along geographic, product market or functional lines; it is characterised by flat hierarchical management, with local flexibility enabling autonomous decisions. By contrast, growing organisations are more likely to impose a mechanistic structure which is bureaucratic, task orientated and dominated by many levels of hierarchical management. If entrepreneurship is to be encouraged and continually supported, leaders need to consider the effects of structural changes over time and be cognisant of the direction that the organisation is travelling between these two extremes. Sine, Mitsuhashi and Kirsch[5] discuss the dilemma that exists as an organisation grows; in order to overcome liabilities of newness, formal structure is critical to reduce role ambiguity and uncertainty. New recruits cannot easily be accommodated unless the rules are known and there is a formal reporting structure in which to operate. However, this sets a direction of travel towards greater hierarchy which becomes increasingly difficult to reverse.

In summary, organisational structure cannot be fixed because environmental conditions, both internal and external, constantly change. As a delicate balance is required we propose that managers use the framework shown in Figure 4.2 as a guide to ensure that as the organisation changes, they do not fall into the trap of creating stagnation and inertia. (See also Morris, Kuratko and Covin (2010).) Ultimately, change can be traumatic; if entrepreneurship is maintained, however, it can be a source of competitive advantage, as we see in the following section.

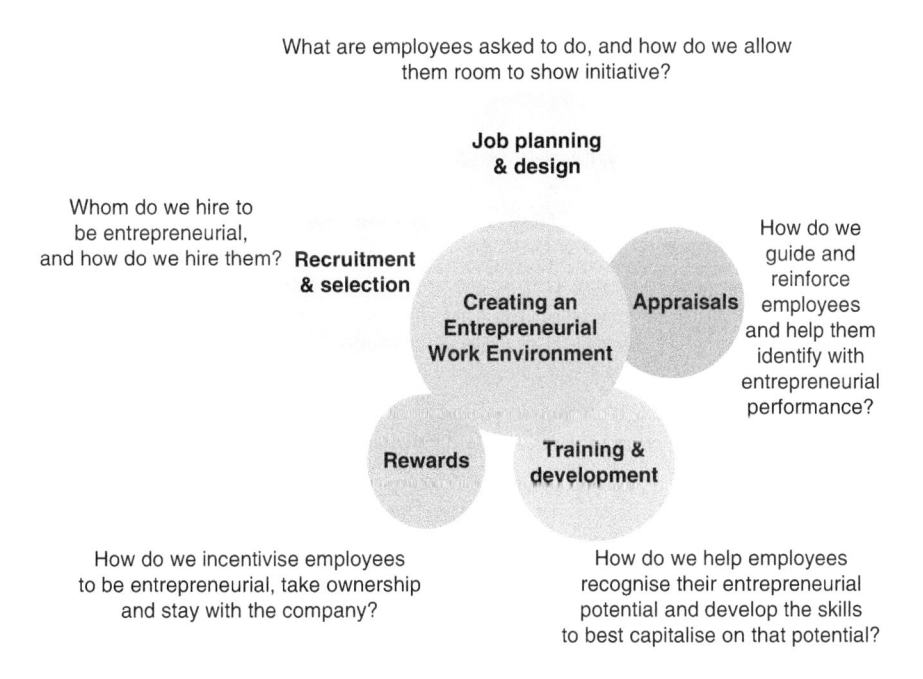

Figure 4.2 Questioning human resource practices for recruiting and rewarding entrepreneurial behaviours.

Source: adapted from Morris, Kuratko and Covin (2010).

4.3 Processes for entrepreneurship

Within an organisation, both tacit and explicit processes can support or hinder entrepreneurship.[6] Barringer and Bluedorn[7] considered the link between entrepreneurial intensity and strategic management practices and found that successful organisations exhibited the following four dimensions to create a supportive environment for entrepreneurial activity:

- **Scanning intensity** – continuous activity to learn about events and trends in the environment.
- **Planning flexibility** – capacity of a firm's strategic plan to change as opportunities/threats emerge.
- **Locus of planning** – depth of employee involvement in a firm's strategic-planning activities.
- **Strategic controls** – base performance on strategically relevant criteria; capable of rewarding creativity, pursuit of opportunities and innovation.

The strategic processes highlighted above aid an organisation in supporting entrepreneurial activity within its boundaries. However, these are just a small part of the many different types of processes that may exist within an organisation that can control approaches to innovation, either by supporting or constraining. Processes can be intentional or unintentionally applied, overtime policies, ways of doing things – and traditions become embedded in the organisation and are continued with little thought as to why they are in place. As a result, processes can be formal or informal in the way they regulate what people do and how they use resources. Consequently, managers need to consider carefully how such processes are applied. For example, financial processes have a role to play in any organisation to ensure financial stability through monitoring how money is spent and how cash is controlled. But financial processes that control do not always support or encourage entrepreneurial activity that can often be contrary to financial aims, with innovation carrying risk and uncertainty. Behavioural processes can often be used to positive effect as they focus upon regulating activity to maintain and sustain desired actions. These processes can also be used to evaluate people's performance in terms of where and how they can be developed. By contrast, setting goals and measuring achievements through output control can help to track performance.

The key when setting and measuring goals, however, is to consider what it is you are asking for and what you are measuring and ensuring that they are aligned – if not, then an organisation runs the risk of encouraging behaviour it does not wish to have. The nature of processes and control should guide development and not be used to punish mistakes. A focus upon removing failures will lead to processes that undoubtedly will inhibit innovation; therefore, once the desired outcomes and expected practices have been decided, they should be built into current processes.

For example, Procter & Gamble's SIMPL (Simplified Initiative Management and Product Launch) product development process has built-in deliverables or 'endpoints' captured within written templates and defined for each stage of their stage-gate process – the project team are thereby aware of what is expected at each of its stages. The SIMPL process goes further in building in the desired and expected practices through defining 'current best approaches' representing standards of performance; these offer suggestions to the leader of the project of which approaches the project should follow (for an example of the process, see Cooper & Mills[8]).

In summary, processes are required as without them uncertainty and ambiguity can inhibit the direction of the organisation, creating confusion. An optimal balance of processes is the key, but this can be difficult to achieve. The processes that are put in place should therefore encourage entrepreneurial behaviours and highlight expected outcomes without seeking to completely remove the possibility of failure which is an inevitable by-product of entrepreneurship (see Chapter 7 for more on failure).

4.4 People: recruiting and rewarding for entrepreneurship

Without question, the people within the organisation are its most valuable resource, especially when considering entrepreneurship. It is important to consider the entrepreneurial role that individuals should take within the organisation and to consider how they can be best supported to ensure they deliver for the organisation. Here we express the view that people should be at the creative heart of the enterprise. Rather than seeing people as vital to innovation and entrepreneurial activity, a cynical view is commonly seen in organisations that operate as if people are part of the problem rather than the key to its solution.

Entrepreneurship calls for proactive human resources practices; a wealth of research demonstrates that every individual has the capability to find and solve complex problems and where such creative behaviour can be harnessed amongst a group of people with differing skills and perspectives extraordinary things can be achieved.[9] This is further enhanced when teamwork is at the centre of innovation. Creativity when combined across different disciplines utilising different perspectives can be extremely powerful. How can organisations solve complex environmental problems such as reducing car emissions if they do not incorporate people from across all different disciplines? Diversity enables innovation to be approached from different perspectives, allowing for powerful combinations of solutions to be exploited.[10] However, most human resource practices discourage interaction outside single-discipline job descriptions.

Pfeffer and Veiga[11] note the strong correlation between proactive human resource practices and the performance of firms in a variety of sectors. Therefore, where knowledge is the driver of competitive advantage and creativity is required to make leaps in our knowledge and understanding, human capital is crucial. The challenge is how to manage individuals in the most effective way so that the organisation is built on the foundations where innovation can flourish. In the following sections we therefore consider the key areas of, first, how you recruit entrepreneurial individuals into the organisation and, second, how you retain them and help them to develop their human capital.

4.4.1 Recruiting the right people for entrepreneurship

When developing an entrepreneurial strategy, organisational growth is often the desired outcome. Yet growth relies on recruiting the right people to maintain and enhance the vision, mission and culture of the organisation desired by its leaders. Therefore, careful thought has to be put into human resource practices, starting at the point of recruitment and selection – considering who the organisation wishes to hire and how you might do so. For instance, Steve Leach from Bigmouthmedia demonstrated a novel and exciting approach. Knowing that he wanted individuals that would be entrepreneurial in their approach to sales he designed the recruitment process to highlight this capability. He developed unusual practices such as asking potential candidates to sell their own shoes as part of the interview process.[12] This might all sound somewhat unorthodox but Steve had highlighted the type of characteristics that people who worked for Bigmouthmedia would need in order to help deliver the firm's entrepreneurial growth. Therefore he designed the recruitment process to consider the skills that potential employees would have to demonstrate at the selection process. This had the double benefit of ensuring that the potential employee was right for Bigmouthmedia and allowing the employees to experience whether Bigmouthmedia was right for them.

A key question to consider, therefore, is whether an organisation's recruitment process searches for the skills necessary to deliver against its entrepreneurial strategy.

4.4.2 Rewarding individuals for entrepreneurial behaviour

In addition to the recruitment and selection, a priority has to be placed on what the individual is going to do through appropriate role planning and design. Netflix, the extremely fast-growing video-streaming service, manages this in an unusually parsimonious manner. Here managers are responsible for defining a new role, yet employees are given complete freedom as how to manage and when they complete their job. There is no policy for hours of work, no policy on annual leave, no salary structure (individuals are appointed with prevailing upper-quartile market rates) and no annual performance reviews. Clearly this is very low cost in terms of the administrative and management time usually deployed in reviewing, capturing, policing and evaluating job performance. According to Netflix CEO Reed Hastings,[13] it also quickly self-selects the individuals who are able to deliver the aggressive growth aspirations of the organisation:

> Adequate performance gets a generous severance package.

Entrepreneurial culture and leadership 53

The stated focus at Netflix is on high performance, freedom and responsibility; the onus is on employing highly qualified and motivated individuals who are capable of managing themselves, with human resource practices designed to be consistent with their entrepreneurial vision and mission.[14]

For organisations that wish to retain the practice of performance review, a key question is how do you appraise people in a way that encourages entrepreneurial behaviour? This links back to some of the earlier arguments around processes and assessing what it is the organisation wishes to measure. This should drive the targets that are set in both the organisation and the appraisal. For the appraisal system to be effective and help to deliver entrepreneurial outcomes it should be linked to employee development and appropriate training and development opportunities within the organisation. When attempting to encourage innovation and entrepreneurial behaviour it can be challenging to ascertain what the incentives should be. Often organisations choose to stay away from financial rewards as they are considered difficult to administer, with the idea generator being far removed from the final innovation. Instead organisations employ peer-reviewed recognition schemes. For instance, Rolls-Royce, the aerospace engine manufacturer, awards the Sir Henry Royce award for technical innovation. Although of limited financial value, this award is highly sought after by employees as it is voted for by their peers and presented at a public ceremony.

In summary, human resource practices need to be designed to recruit and reward individuals to deliver the entrepreneurial strategy of the organisation. By asking the questions in Figure 4.2, managers can examine their practices across different areas to establish whether their current practices are fit for the required purpose or whether they need to be redesigned.

We have considered examples of supportive human resource practices from Netflix as it sought to grow rapidly through entrepreneurship and those of Rolls-Royce, for whom technical innovation is key. In Chapter 5 we consider those practices adopted by Unilever as it aimed to grow through developing more sustainable products globally. Clearly practices are context and agency specific but the following normative list can be helpful for managers as they reconcile their entrepreneurial strategy with incumbent human resource policies and procedures.[15]

- Appropriate use of rewards: an effective reward system should spur entrepreneurial activity; consider goals, feedback, emphasis on individual responsibility and incentives. Rewards can be motivational but, more important, signal what people should be doing in terms of entrepreneurial behaviours.
- Management support: top managers must lead by example if people further down the organisation are to trust their initiative; this includes championing, providing resources and expertise and institutionalising entrepreneurship.
- Resource availability: time must be allocated or made available for entrepreneurial activity; employees must perceive their availability; availability encourages experimentation and risk taking.

- Supportive administrative structure: make sure supportive administrative processes are in place by which ideas are evaluated, chosen and implemented; they must be efficient and effective to demonstrate that ideas can become realities.
- Risk-tolerance: encourage risk-taking and tolerate failure; emphasis on learning from mistakes or negative events; practices must not punish negative outcomes.

4.5 Entrepreneurial leadership

Any organisation requires key individuals to aid and support the entrepreneurial and innovative process. The history of successful innovation is scattered with exceptional characters who combine energy and creative insight to invent and carry forward new concepts. Steve Jobs, Larry Page, Sergey Brin and Richard Branson top most Google searches for entrepreneurial leaders. Empirical research, however, identifies a number of less-heralded leadership roles that are critical for innovative outcomes.

For successful innovation internal technical resources and communication channels are vital, but of equal importance is information from the external environment.[16] Diverse external inputs into any development project are required from multiple sources, including suppliers, users, competitors, government agencies and universities. For such communication and boundary-spanning activity to be effective it has to be facilitated by key individuals (internal to the organisation) commonly known as gatekeepers. Such gatekeepers have been conceptualised in various ways including boundary-spanners, key communicators, communication stars and linking-pins.[17] Tushman and Katz[18] argue that individuals partaking in such activity 'are capable of understanding and translating contrasting coding schemes' (p. 1072). Defined as highly communicative they act as a link-pin with the capacity to be 'high internal and external communicators who are able to effectively transfer external ideas and information into their project groups'[19] (p16). Gatekeepers, however, can be more than translators of information between the external and internal environment. Singh and Fleming[20] (2010) argue that they tend to increase a company's inventive creativity through their ability to adopt and adapt others' new combinations – they are more likely to develop radical concepts.

Other influential roles supporting innovation within the organisation have been captured through empirical research. The presence of an innovation champion has been linked to the success of innovation projects. Champions are individuals that emerge to support an innovation through making 'a decisive contribution to the innovation by actively and enthusiastically promoting its progress through the critical [organisational] stages'.[21] The issue here is that organisational systems and procedures developed in large companies are usually designed to maintain the status quo and avoid risks. To overcome this inertia a credible champion is necessary to sell the idea to senior management to get them sufficiently interested in the project.[22] Champions achieve such buy-in from senior management through their intense enthusiasm and interest in the project, which they demonstrate by playing dominant roles in the key events and stages of the innovation process. They are further characterised by their ability to overcome obstacles associated with the project so that, through willpower and determination, the project can overcome institutional barriers to progress.

Empirical research has therefore highlighted the dialectic nature of entrepreneurship within certain organisations where entrepreneurial leaders appear to dictate yet boundary spanners and champions are actually required to change their entrepreneurial aspirations. By contrast, a different approach has been captured where a more democratic process of creating an entrepreneurial vision appears more effective.

4.5.1 Entrepreneurial Vision through Innovation Challenges

A key aspect of entrepreneurial leadership is guiding and shaping the future direction of the organisation. Such a vision for where the organisation is heading is extremely important as it sets the modus operandi,[23] – the way that the organisation operates – and it provides a sense of what the organisation stands for and where it is going. As the organisation grows it is important that this is shared and valued by all in the organisation as it underpins the culture. However, especially if the organisation has adopted an organic structure, it cannot be specified through outcomes; rather, it should be a vision that everyone involved in the organisation must share and feel part of.

Furr and Dyer[24] argue that the creation of a grand innovation challenge is an effective mechanism to create such a shared vision. They cite the example of Steve Jobs, who challenged his team using the slogan '1,000 songs in your pocket' prior to the development of the iPod. Furr and Dyer argue that, just as innovation is about discovery, the role of the leader should be one that involves setting the direction and letting employees find their own way. Rather than 'heroic' leaders espousing the ability to predict what the future might hold, the role should be to specify the innovation space where entrepreneurship is to take place. Furr and Dyer illustrate their point by highlighting Amazon's pursuit of flying drones as a statement to the whole organisation that radical innovation is to be encouraged. Leadership should give confidence to those in the organisation to re-imagine what the future could look like and actively question the core assumptions that the organisation was founded upon.

4.5.2 Challenges of entrepreneurial leadership

Undoubtedly entrepreneurship involves change, which can be perceived as extremely disruptive, risky and costly for all involved. As competencies become developed and ingrained across the organisation, they become 'the way things are done around here'; the organisation develops deep-rooted cognitive behaviours and routines that support how the organisation operates, underpinning the norms and behaviours. Energy, vision and inspiration are required to prevail over the status quo. As growth occurs, organisations can suffer from inertia, where change is no longer the norm, people seek stability and complacency creeps in. The prevalent view can be extremely limiting because, whilst everyone knows where the organisation wishes to go and how they plan on getting there, it can create a certain kind of blindness to what is coming over the horizon in the form of new technologies, products/services offering and competition. This is referred to as peripheral vision. See the following video link: http://viscog.beckman.illinois.edu/flashmovie/15.php; this short video highlights the effects of concentrating on one mission for a period of time and the consequent limitation upon noticing anything unexpected. This is analogous to the situation in which an organisation fails to understand the value of a new invention or way of doing things. For instance, when James Dyson visited Hoover with his concept of a cyclone vacuum cleaner, managers at Hoover were not able to view the world from Dyson's point of view. He saw the advantage to the consumer in greater cleaning functionality, yet Hoover managers could not envisage a business model where there was no requirement for dust-collecting bags, a key revenue stream in their current paradigm. Rather than core competencies being leveraged for future competitive advantage the opposite effect was observed, where core competencies regress and become a core rigidity[25] which hinders the organisation and prevents it from viewing the world differently.

This is where the importance of leadership and top management becomes crucial; leadership must be able to change mind-sets and refocus energy in a way that stimulates change from within and creates a meaningful innovation challenge that is shared across the organisation. Such a challenge for Hoover could have been to explore ways in which the performance of vacuum cleaners could be improved tenfold, for example. This would have been unlikely to be met without challenging the existing paradigm and would have led to a very different reception to radical concepts such as that presented by Dyson.

There is consensus in the literature that leadership is a critical factor affecting innovation. The rationale is that leaders should have significant influence on product innovation because, as individuals, they take the greater share of decision making about organisational strategy and operations.[26] Also as leaders, they have an impact on organisational characteristics such as culture, strategy, structure and reward systems.[27]

As a leader, however, which is the right style to adopt, and how does it differ to management, when the two are used interchangeably? Peter Drucker makes the argument that 'Management is doing things right; leadership is doing the right things.' But this does not help us to understand the type of leadership style that is important to lead an organisation through change and drive innovation. Leadership-style terminology includes *transformational, democratic, charismatic, architectural* – the list goes on, and it is not the intention of this chapter to critically discuss the different styles. In sum, according to Robyn Benincasa,[28] the bottom line is:

> If you take two cups of authoritative leadership, one cup of democratic, coaching, and affiliative leadership, and a dash of pacesetting and coercive

leadership to taste, and you lead based on need in a way that elevates and inspires your team, you've got an excellent recipe for long-term leadership success with every team in your life.

A pragmatic approach is to find a balance between a style that works for the individual and the organisation, and alternating between styles depending on the nature of the task at hand.

4.6 Conclusion: Diagnosis of entrepreneurial culture

In summary, entrepreneurship is often seen as the domain of a few, remaining in the realms of the research and development department or top management. Yet if real competitive success is to be sustained then research shows that entrepreneurship should include everyone.

Underpinning the organisation are the structures, processes and people, which are all inherently interlinked. If one fails, the system as a whole typically fails. Through sustained practice, they all determine the organisational culture, the way that the organisation approaches innovation. Finally, the role of the leader in providing the innovation challenges and empowering employees to create a shared entrepreneurial vision provides the platform from which culture can take over.

This leads to the following questions that can be used to diagnose the entrepreneurial culture of your organisation.

1   How is the organisation structured for entrepreneurship?
2   How are people recruited and rewarded for entrepreneurship?
3   What organisational processes support or constrain entrepreneurship?
4   How are innovation challenges identified?

In Chapter 5 we explore how these questions were addressed within an entrepreneurial multinational, Unilever.

References

1 Greiner, L. (1972). 'Evolution and revolution as organizations grow', *Harvard Business Review*, 50(4): 39–46.
2 Churchill, N. C. & Lewis, V. L. (1983). 'The five stages of small business', *Harvard Business Review*, 61(3): 30–50.
3 Mintzberg, H. (1994). *The Rise and Fall of Strategic Planning: Reconceiving the Roles for Planning, Plans, Planners.* New York: Free Press, p. 458.
4 Burns, T. & Stalker, G. M. (1961). *The Management of Innovation.* London: Tavistock.
5 Sine, W. D., Mitsuhashi H. & Kirsch, D. A. (2006). 'Revisiting Burns and Stalker: Formal structure and new venture performance in emerging economic sectors', *Harvard Business Review*, 49(1): 121–132.
6 Munoz, C., Mosey, S. & Binks, M. (2013). 'The tacit mystery: Reconciling different approaches to tacit knowledge', *Knowledge Management Research and Practice*, 1–10.

7 Barringer, B. R. & Bluedorn, A. C. (1999). 'The relationship between corporate entrepreneurship and strategic management', *Strategic Management Journal*, 20(5): 421–444.
8 Cooper, R. G. & Mills, M. S. (2005). 'Succeeding at new product development the P&G Way: A key element is using the "Innovation Diamond"', *PDMA Visions*, XXIX(4): 9–13.
9 Munoz, C., Mosey, S. & Binks, M. (2011). 'Developing opportunity-identification capabilities in the classroom: Visual evidence for changing mental frames', *Academy of Management Learning and Education*, 10(2): 277–295.
10 Clarysse, B., Mosey, S. & Lambrecht, I. (2009, September). 'New trends in technology management education: A view from Europe', *Academy of Management Learning and Education*, 8(3): 427–443.
11 Pfeffer, J. & Veiga, J. F. (1999). 'Putting people first for organizational success', *Academy of Management Executive*, 13(2): 37–48.
12 Purkayastha, D. (2009). *Bigmouthmedia and Steve Leach: Managing a winning team*. IBS Center for Management Research, 809-030-1.
13 Netflix (2015). Online. Company overview. Available at https://pr.netflix.com/WebClient/loginPageSalesNetWorksAction.do?contentGroupId=1047.
14 Ibid.
15 Hornsby, J. S., Kuratko, D.F. & Zahra, S.A. (2002). 'Middle managers' perception of the internal environment for corporate entrepreneurship: Assessing a measurement scale'. *Journal of Business Venturing*, 17: 49–63.
16 Utterback, J. M. (1971). 'The process of technological innovation within the firm', *Academy of Management*, 14(1): 75–88.
17 Conway, S. (1997). 'Strategic personal links in successful innovation: Link-pins, bridges, and liaisons', *Creativity and Innovation Management*, 6(4): 226–233.
18 Tushman, M.L. & Katz, R. (1980). 'External communication and project performance: An investigation into the role of gatekeepers', *Management Science*, 26(11): 1071–1085.
19 Katz, R. & Allen, T. J. (1983). 'Investigating the Not Invented Here (NIH) syndrome: A look at the performance, tenure, and communication patterns of 50 R & D Project Groups', *R&D Management*, 12(1): 7–20.
20 Singh, J. & Fleming, L. (2010). 'Lone inventors as sources of breakthroughs: Myth or reality?', *Management Science*, 56(1): 41–56.
21 Achilladelis, B., Jervis, P. & Robertson, A. (1971). *A Study of Success and Failure in Industrial Innovation*. Eastbourne, Sussex, UK: Sussex Academic Press, p. 14.
22 Chakrabarti, A. K. (1974). 'The role of champion in product innovation', *California Management Review*, XVII(2): 58–62.
23 Ireland, R.D., Covin, J.G. & Kuratko, D.F. (2009). 'Conceptualizing corporate entrepreneurship strategy', *Entrepreneurship Theory and Practice*, 33(1): 19–46.
24 Furr, N. R. & Dyer, J. H. (2014). 'Leading your team into the unknown', *Harvard Business Review*, 92(12): 80–88.
25 Leonard-Barton, D. (1992). 'Core capabilities and core rigidities: A paradox in managing new product development', *Strategic Management Journal*, 13 (summer): 111–125.
26 Hambrick, D. (2007). 'Upper echelon theory: Revisited', *Academy of Management Review*, 32(2): 334–343.
27 Cummings, L.L. & O'Connell, M.J. (1978). 'Organizational innovation: A model and needed research', *Journal of Business Research*, 6(1): 33–50.
28 Benincasa, R. (2012). *How Winning Works: Eight Essential Leadership Lessons from the Toughest Teams on Earth*. Don Mills, ON, Canada: Harlequin Nonfiction, p. 170.

5 Building a culture of entrepreneurship in practice

Jim Crilly, Hannah Noke and Paul Kirkham

5.1 Introduction

This chapter is concerned with how organisations build a culture of entrepreneurship in practice. We draw upon a series of interviews with Jim Crilly, Senior Vice President for Research at Unilever, in which he shared his personal views of the leadership and culture required to stimulate entrepreneurship within large organisations. We reflect upon his experience of a time when Unilever radically restructured its business through selling off major global brands that had stagnated and subsequently refocused upon those with the most growth potential. We explain how Unilever identified the need for a change in culture to revitalise the business and the structural changes and new recruitment and reward practices it introduced to stimulate this change. We highlight the role of leadership in nurturing and supporting entrepreneurship and summarise how Unilever addressed innovation challenges to embed entrepreneurship as 'the way things are done around here' across different functions and geographic regions.

5.2 The importance of an entrepreneurial culture

We begin by considering the importance of entrepreneurial culture.[1] Jim explains why, for him, it is pivotal to entrepreneurship and innovation, through recounting a story told by Professor Ranjay Gulati of Harvard Business School, who presented at Unilever's annual Change Leaders Conference in 2013. Although it's a story outside of Jim's field and Unilever's industry, it is one that resonated with him and illustrates the important role of culture in terms of appropriate leadership, structures and processes to create the freedom to look beyond the obvious:

> The Salinas Valley in California grows around 70 per cent of the USA's lettuce, superb lettuce, all year round quality. So the producers continually go to their customers and they say 'how can we be better, what else can we do with our lettuce?' And maybe they want them bigger, or greener, or rounder; and of course they'd like a longer shelf life. All incremental

improvements – I mean, how can you be radical with a lettuce! But all of a sudden the market is taken apart. A new development that didn't come from a lettuce producer, it didn't come from farming, nor did it come from the scientists and it didn't come from the retailer. Where do you think it came from? Packaging. Their insight was that working women, working men, when they come home, don't want to be bothered taking a lettuce out and cutting it and then taking another lettuce, cutting it and putting in some basil or whatever. So this development has revolutionised the lettuce business, bagged salad, because that is what consumers need and not just in the USA but everywhere – you have seen the rows and rows of different mixes etc. It was bang on for meeting the consumers' unmet needs. And the thing is that this product is far more cost effective than head lettuce: it uses the smaller and misshapen heads that might have been left in the fields, it takes less labour to maintain on the shelves, and it can be kept there for longer thanks to its packaging.

This innovation arose from asking the right questions, seeking the right insight and targeting the innovation on real unmet needs;[2] in Salinas Valley, they found an unmet need. The insight and identification of the need arose from the understanding that in our fast-paced world, people have a wish to eat healthy food, but the problem is time spent in preparing and washing salad. People are concerned with being able to have their salad ready and pre-prepared in the mix they desire. For this convenience they are prepared to pay a premium, as Jim exclaims: 'Remarkably, in that sense lettuce has become a premium product!' Yet, the innovation did not come in the usual form of product innovation via the usual channels of marketing or R&D – it came as a packaging innovation. Yet because the lettuce growers in Salinas Valley were open to new insights and ideas, they could see the opportunity. This story reflects the culture that Unilever aspired to create at the time of its restructuring, as Jim explains:

> The reason I tell you this story is that it is atypical – Unilever is one of the world's leading suppliers of Food, Home and Personal Care products with sales in over 190 countries. We work with 174,000 colleagues around the world and generated annual sales of €49.8 billion in 2013, and this didn't come about by good luck. Certainly we have to be able to seize ideas that come out of the blue but we can't rely on them. We need to build a culture of entrepreneurship across the whole organisation. Oh, and by the way, that bagged lettuce innovation didn't come to the packagers by pure chance either – it came from a deep understanding of the consumer, asking the right questions about customers' needs and wants, doing the right research, carefully studying peoples' lives and the problems they face every day. Hard work, not good luck.

One of the key questions for those wishing to create an entrepreneurial organisation to support innovation and growth within their business is how do large organisations do it? How do they create entrepreneurial cultures that support innovation despite their size? In the late 1980s Unilever had to address these questions as they faced deficits in growth and a lack of innovation in key areas. As a result, the company embarked upon a series of initiatives to understand its underperformance, gathering and analysing critical performance data in order to appreciate what it was not doing or not doing well. Jim was asked to co-lead a project on R&D in innovation, causing him to question, 'How do the best innovators manage R&D and technology development to get growth?' One of the tools Jim and his team employed was benchmarking, pioneered by the US company Xerox. Implemented as part of a larger approach known as Total Quality Management (TQM), benchmarking[3] is the process of identifying companies that are best at a given generic process/activity, studying how the best in class do it and how well they do it. Jim's task was to benchmark and compare the best-in-class companies with Unilever's internal equivalents to find the gaps. Then Jim and his team were able to put in place an improvement plan. Jim emphasises that benchmarking can work either internally or externally and it can work on best in class at the company level, industrial sector or even functional or generic level. The benchmarking process implemented within Unilever was composed of the following three steps:

1. Conducting a deep literature scan to find out what's been reported about companies in relevant journals and forming a view of which companies are the benchmarks for which processes.
2. Interacting with successful companies, examining what they do in technological innovation and learning their practices and processes.
3. Bringing these ideas back to Unilever.

Jim reflects on the critical nature of the visits to the companies Unilever used as a benchmark:

> We needed to understand how the processes were woven into the cultural and organisational fabric of the company – context was crucial. TQM gave companies a neutral banner under which to meet and compare processes all in the interest of mutual-performance improvement ambitions. And so we were able to interchange with companies like 3M, IBM, Xerox, Bell Laboratories, Motorola – none of them from our own sector. Personally and professionally, I learned a lot and took back some very valuable insights. Benchmarking back then inspired several of the processes Unilever uses today. For example, we learned roadmapping from the world leader in the technique, Motorola. And in return they learned our approach to consumer research and product testing. I recall clearly that in those days everyone's benchmark for innovation excellence was the Minnesota Mining and Manufacturing Company (The 3M Company). They seemed to do it all really well – strategy, processes, creativity, technology management, but what stood out most of all was their culture.

That was over 20 years ago and they're still admired. Of course these days Google and Apple have become 'top of the leaguers' for creativity and innovation at company level but many of their principles and practices are very reminiscent of those which I first encountered at 3M and others years ago.

We will revisit 3M in more detail in Chapter 9, but returning to Unilever's approach, following the benchmarking exercise they codified their findings within a booklet that was circulated across the organisation. This document highlighted the need for changes in practice across the following three areas:

1 Building New Understanding – a deeper consciousness of what Unilever knew about itself and its customers. An awareness of trends – where the consumers were going, where the technologies were going.
2 Finding New Angles – developing the creative mindset that finds new perspectives from inside and outside the company.
3 Nurturing New Ideas – recognising that innovation can be seen as unnecessary, costly, risky or irrelevant. The potential of new insights is easy to miss – to thrive they nearly always need time, space and encouragement.
4 Keeping the momentum going - continuous improvement; refining and improving the processes over the years.

5.3 Structuring for entrepreneurship and identifying innovation challenges

Unilever concluded that for such entrepreneurial practices to be realised, an appropriate structure had to be created. Company leaders subsequently set up innovation centres, dedicated to certain parts of categories and businesses, providing resources dedicated to innovation to particular brands in particular parts of the world. Often entrepreneurship can be seen to be in contrast with the need for systems and structure,[4] yet they are essential in a large corporation, especially in a multinational, because there are so many barriers to generating new and appropriate ideas. Jim explains that a key role of structure is to provide direction and focus:

> One approach is to say 'just give me your ideas, we will put up a suggestion box or website and you can give us your ideas'. Well then you get lots of ideas but 95 per cent of them are pretty useless because they are all over the place. So we learned that 'ab initio' we have to give people direction, focus and stimulus. 'I want ideas in this area to meet those sorts of consumer needs with these types of technologies'. You get fewer ideas but the quality is much higher. We have learned to distinguish between these two approaches. We call the first spontaneous – it's anywhere, anyone and anytime. Packaged salad is that sort of spontaneous innovation. The second one we call stimulated, and usually stimulated ideas come out

of a workshop or event where we have come together to discuss new developments, trends etc.

Jim's example highlights that it is the process of asking for ideas within the scope of an 'innovation challenge' that Unilever found to be the most effective. A particularly effective way of stimulating innovation within Unilever was to issue an innovation challenge to a team or, more broadly, whilst simultaneously sharing the entrepreneurial vision. The process of defining the challenge in itself was deliberately defined to be stretching so it could not be tackled alone. It required the involvement of others, such as consumers, to ask them about their problems, observe them and look at what they required to meet their unmet needs. It would require additional outside presence in the form of outside systems to harness the power of the external world. Jim explains the power of such open innovation approaches: 'Nowadays you put up a bubble: "Has anyone solved the problem of making soap with 5 per cent less water?" Bang! – you have lots of answers back very quickly.' By contrast, Jim reflects on the vast difference social media and approaches to open innovation have meant to innovation:

> In the 1980s we didn't have Facebook or Twitter but we did have a very effective network. We had internal contacts – people who knew each other from right across the company in different functions, regions and locations. Unilever has a strongly connected network – people stay a long time, they get to know each other and they know who to go to. But building that network takes leadership, it takes time – it doesn't happen overnight.

Jim provides an in-depth and thought provoking example of how these challenges and networks integrate from start to finish across the diverse corporate context:

> Like all great innovations it starts with a great idea – a technical possibility – to meet a real consumer unmet need. That need was all about reducing wrinkles around the eyes, which is particularly a desire for post-menopausal women. The idea was the brainchild of two Unilever scientists who were convinced that a nutritional formulation which can promote the right gene signalling to boost collagen biosynthesis would deliver an effective solution. Now this was a particularly challenging innovation as it fell in between two major Unilever categories – Foods and Personal Care – and the struggle was that this product didn't make an easy fit with either. Clearly, the benefit was a personal care one, but the product format required oral delivery. It was never going to be a favourite for either category, therefore not to be prioritised and resourced fully. And yet the science was great and the benefit powerfully proven in an extensive clinical trial. So, the next real challenge was going to be how to make this innovation happen. It was left to the informal network of people in the

64 *Building an Entrepreneurial Organisation*

company who believed in the science, believed in the concept, and finally got it there to prove the concept and the business model. And the way it finally got to market was via a small start-up company called Spa Salon International – a part Unilever-owned venture company specialising in beauty treatments, which had a need to innovate during a downturn in their core business.

The result of this challenge-led approach was that it motivated people, giving them purpose in which to find ideas and goals that they could contribute personally and collectively. Having structure therefore appears to be vital in helping find the 'right' idea, but Jim argues that not only structure but also people are key to the process; specifically people trained in teamworking, creative thinking and, in Unilever's case, consumer insight. For Jim, one of the most insightful leaders of the creative culture in the 1980s was Akio Morita of Sony, whom he recalls speaking at a government-sponsored lecture in London in 1992[5] about the role of innovation challenges:

> The innovation process does not begin by bubbling up from the research and development laboratory, or from brainstorming sessions by the product planners. The innovation process begins with a mandate which must be set at the highest levels of the corporation by identifying goals and priorities; and once identified, these must be communicated all the way down the line. The targets you set must be clear and challenging because you cannot wait for innovation to just show up at your company one day. But you need not, and should not, possess the entire solution to the challenge you set. You just have to be sure that the target you raise is realistic, though it might appear impossible.

In Jim's experience, over time more and more people see the sense and the logic behind these principles and they promulgate them and put them into practice. Within a big enterprise Jim explains how it is vital that all stakeholders are on board; one 'no' from somewhere and the time and effort invested in the project will have been wasted. In a similar vein as with individual entrepreneurs; those who have got ideas need to be able to sell those ideas. As a result, Unilever incorporated corporate entrepreneurs into the process to encourage and enthuse engagement. Company leaders found commitment to be vital to the innovation process within Unilever, finding a way to sell an idea so people will be motivated and active. Storytelling was prescribed as a core capability for every would-be innovator; ideas within Unilever were therefore pitched to the senior leaders to explain the latent opportunities inherent in any particular innovation. It became increasingly important for those doing the pitching to find the right way to get the message across convincingly. Rather than focusing on data-led approaches that had been traditionally employed, Jim encouraged his team to use samples and 'NORPs' (non-optimised research prototypes) to provide meaningful images and great storytelling. Jim steered people away from becoming fixated on equations and complex figures. He advocated the ability to get the message across in simple language, via media which resonated with customers and potential sponsors. Pitching became viewed as an extremely important skill and the development of that capability was actively promoted.

5.4 Recruiting the right people for entrepreneurship

In addition to developing the capabilities of existing employees, another key consideration for building an entrepreneurial culture at Unilever was how to recruit the right people for entrepreneurship. Jim makes a case that innovation thrives in a diverse environment, one where it is not always easy to hire or develop entrepreneurial people. He draws on the work of Leonard and Straus[6] who present the argument that 'to innovate successfully you must hire, work with and promote people who are unlike you'.[7] In Jim's interview he was keen to stress the importance of diversity for Unilever:

> It is very important that you have diversity – in a function, in a team and in a company. Diversity in background and personality, diversity in discipline, diversity in gender and so on. You need a mix of different people with different skills and different attitudes, and if you don't have enough diversity you will struggle to do really new things because everything will default to the status quo. You need to recruit people who are not like you.

Jim further expands on the concept of diversity by arguing that creativity should be viewed as an attribute that is scalable; it may well start with creative individuals but it should and can work at the level of the team and cohorts and in fact every organisational stratum even up to the entire enterprise.

One of the fundamental issues in Jim's discussion was how to build on people's creativity and how to develop individuals who are prepared to encourage the creativity of others and also encourage entrepreneurship. Within Jim's role as Senior Vice President for Research, he felt that it was about setting up the right team; for him, that could be the right composition of functions, but importantly, the emphasis was on the right combination of individuals:

> that means making sure you have a few shapers but you also need completers, finishers, or the project will not get landed in accordance with Belbin.[8] The shapers will still be spinning the plates, thinking and developing new options leaving others to plan and drive progress. And if you don't have somebody there to make it happen against a plan with a clear endpoint then it just doesn't happen.

In Unilever's fast-moving consumer goods (FMCGs), one of the key requirements is continuous innovation – a steady stream of new products to fill the shelves. Hence, Jim argues: 'Culture, values and consumers are always mentioned at Unilever, supported by training, tools and techniques. This doesn't always come easily. Some people are very lucky and seem to have it in their genes but very often you need training'.

In tandem with recruiting the right people and providing stimulating training and development, Jim suggests that 'freedom' is a key enabler for entrepreneurial activity. Providing a feeling of freedom to think entrepreneurially enabled Unilever to capitalise on the deliberate diversity it sought. It was able to bring together different inputs and perspectives from those individuals that had been painstakingly chosen to be part of a team. Such entrepreneurial freedom facilitated people to diverge and explore new possibilities, especially in the early stages of a project. Jim explains how the purposeful diversity aided in some cases:

> Sometimes when we can't find a solution to this problem through the way we are going, we say: 'let's see if we can diverge and bring some people in'. We call them creative 'interlopers' – people who are deliberately brought in to stimulate divergent thinking.

5.5 Supporting and rewarding entrepreneurship

In Jim's experience, entrepreneurial freedom on its own will not deliver innovation success; rather, it has to be supported by leadership to provide direction and guidance regarding where the creativity should be applied. He highlights three contrasting management styles and approaches that he observed to yield very different innovative outcomes amongst teams:

1. Laissez faire – the manager who does not get involved; 'just get on with it and report back at the end of the year'.
2. Directive style – 'When I want your opinion, I will give it to you'.
3. Participative – the manager who works *with* people, facilitating, sponsoring and supporting individuals.

From the three styles highlighted, Jim explains that company leaders at Unilever believed successful management was achieved through adopting a participative management style as it 'really embraces and nourishes creativity and innovation'. However, Jim strikes a note of warning: it is essential that the style of management be aligned with the requirements of the company itself. For instance, the latitude to be able to handle the mavericks, people Jim defines as those who do not quite fit the management norm:

> Mavericks by definition find management and administration tasks a drag. When they are in a meeting they are often thinking about something else. And yet if you want a new idea that's the very person who'll give you it – that is where their real value lies.

Mavericks thrive on challenges, autonomy and freedom, yet they all require leadership to provide direction and focus. If a certain management style does not let this happen, they get very frustrated; the risk is they either become unproductive or leave the company.

Jim provides us with a useful reminder that leadership can make or break a company; it can enhance innovation or inhibit it. Jim reflects that leadership and management behaviour are really the key determinant of creativity and resolve in an enterprise:

> Management support and openness: leaders have to model the behaviour they want. Remember all those functions: supply chain, finance and marketing – if the heads of those functions do not let their people talk to each other, we are never going to get horizontal engagement. Leadership must always be thinking about the future whilst at the same time not taking their eye off the ball of current business performance.

This is the paradox of management in an innovative company. Jim articulates this as 'out of the box' creativity and 'in the box' development. For Jim, it was about finding a balance rather than viewing it as a conflict, as he explains: 'because in a portfolio company of brands and products, incremental innovation is needed to keep the business ticking over at the same time as radical innovation is being developed to establish new business platforms'. Applying the concept of ambidexterity,[9] any organisation that wishes to survive has to be able to be able to carry out both forms of innovation simultaneously, where the process of doing both is equally as natural as the other. In Jim's words:

> There are two distinct aspects of innovation – the creative phase followed by the productive phase. People often confuse these aspects – they think creativity is innovation and innovation is creativity – but they are two distinct phases of essentially the same business process. Imagination leads to the idea and then the idea is turned into reality, but it's very much one process – envisioning the future.

Jim is keen to explain that the process of innovation as it is described may seem like organised chaos, a mix of different things, as if describing two different companies. Rather, it describes the management values, the management style that is needed to support creative thinking and risk taking in an enterprise that wants to grasp a long-term future. It reflects the complexity of the entrepreneurial process and the differences required at different stages of the innovation process. 3M describes its culture as organised chaos,[10] reflecting the need for chaos to stimulate the creativity required and then the organisation, the discipline to convert creativity and develop the ideas in order to deliver value to the market.

A timeless question regarding innovation in large and small organisations alike is how should you reward innovation. Jim's approach to this question is rather different as he comes from the position of understanding what motivates researchers and innovators. He is keen to distinguish between intrinsic and extrinsic motivations. Jim explains that, from his experience, by far the most influential are intrinsic factors such as the freedom to work on interesting and purposeful projects, peer recognition and appreciation and the chance to work with a wide range of stimulating colleagues. These are closely followed the freedom to take risks and nonconformity. Somewhat counterintuitively, less-influential factors are the extrinsic rewards such as salary and other monetary remuneration. As Jim points out, people want a fair return on their labour but the evidence is that salary alone is rarely a deal breaker. In his experience, the key motivators are autonomy and freedom and tolerance of failure in the pursuit of ambitious challenges. It is the tolerance of failure that Jim also sees as a key indicator regarding the company's culture:

> If you go in and say what happened to so and so when that project failed and if you find that they were fired, asked to leave, or just disappeared – okay, you will know it's not a very forgiving culture – not a very conducive climate. In 3M I heard this slogan: 'you have to kiss 1,000 frogs to find a prince'; and another: 'failure is accepted as a necessary part of learning'.

It is within such a supportive culture that people are more likely to be well disposed to innovative thinking – trying new things – with an enterprising attitude and not inhibited by the fear of failure. For Jim, 'I've come to realise that fear of failure is probably the biggest single inhibitor of innovation in a company.'

5.6 Integrating leadership, processes and structure

When asked 'how do these process, structure and leadership combine to build an entrepreneurial culture?' Jim provides a considered reply:

> I am a scientist and I shouldn't say that I sense something when I don't have sensors to do it, but what I'm speaking about here is more like intuition. When you visit a company, even just when you're waiting in reception, you sense the atmosphere. It is like a sixth sense – you get the gist of what sort of company you're visiting. In an innovative atmosphere you say to yourself this place is energetic, people are purposeful and there are things going on here.

Jim consistently uses the descriptor of 'climate' as distinct from 'culture' when reflecting upon entrepreneurship at Unilever. Culture, for Jim, described the values of the company, what it believes in through the deep-seated attitudes established over a long period of time. Climate was more about management style and behaviour, understanding motivation and how people feel about the way they are treated, as Jim explains:

> You have got a great idea but your manager stays in his office and closes the door. Say they walk straight past when they meet you in the corridor.

Do you think that is going to promote creativity and innovation? No. So that is what we are getting at. Accessibility of management, particularly senior leaders of people who are creative – those engaged in the creative process. People are more likely to propose ideas if they believe the leader expects it and is accessible to them.

This for Jim reinforces Akio Morita's lecture in which he stated that everybody in the company should participate in innovation. Morita included the blue-collar workers, the people who come in and who do not believe they are paid to have ideas. They believe they are paid to use their hands, do the job and go home. Jim states:

> I'm with Morita – we say 'No, we want you to use your brains and respond to our challenges'. You must realise that if you are in a leading role it is important to let people know you expect their ideas and you are going to contribute your own – participative management.

Clearly, leaders need to model the behaviour they want from everybody else. And then, when they gain a reputation as being a creative and innovative and forward-looking company, it becomes self-sustaining:

> You create a lot of talent and you attract a lot of talent. You have to remember this attribute is not just about the company of today; it's for bringing in the talent of the future. So you see that creativity can be learned, it works at the individual level, it works at the team level and it works at the company level.

In order for entrepreneurship to be present, then, business leaders of Unilever found that they had to overcome the paradox of managing entrepreneurship, dealing with 'loose-tight management'.[11] This meant dealing with the contradiction of encouraging freedom to explore at certain times and requiring tight discipline involving highly professional project management at other times, with a cross-functional project team and a well-defined process with stages and gates which ensure risk and time are rigorously managed to hit a predefined launch date. For Unilever this was a case of building new structures and processes to manage this paradox. As described earlier, the early stages of the innovation process are characterised by divergent thinking, freedom and diversity, yet Jim recognises that:

> Innovation is an end to end very complex process – there's an upstream and a downstream and we need to know where we are and take the appropriate management approach. Upstream is event driven whereas the downstream is time driven because there's a deadline. Downstream is a phase of the innovation that needs discipline and process. When you are dealing with the biggest retailers in the world, where dependability is critical, if you say you will launch a new product in the Spring next year

then that has to happen. So when things are time driven, instead of patience, you have a sense of urgency.

For Unilever, it has taken 20 years to develop its innovation process. Today, it is a very well-defined and documented process that is practiced company-wide. It has had to be fully underpinned by a powerful global system that comes with its own personality, even with bespoke branding as IPM™ (Innovation Process Management). The upstream-ideas phase focuses on creating new opportunities as distinct from the downstream process of bringing an innovation to the market. This suggests it is a very sequential end-to-end process but that would be a bit of a simplification. Ideas do not always go straight into the innovation pipeline but get reviewed and recycled perhaps several times – some are kept alive by a keen proponent, others become sequestered in Unilever's innovation larder where the company believes in 'thou shalt not kill an idea' as adopted from 3M. Jim expresses the need for persistence and tenacity in the innovator:

> I think there's a seven-year cycle: 'Oh we worked on that seven years ago, it didn't seem to work.' And then, lo and behold the old idea comes back in vogue. What you have to avoid saying to people is that it won't work – 'its time will come'. Really great ideas will stand the test of time. They may come prematurely or at the wrong time but they will find their way with the support of a champion in the company.

Therefore some spontaneous ideas may be around for quite some time before their potential can be realised as: 'things pop up and they also disappear spontaneously'. This is described as 'event driven' at Unilever; Jim talks about the need for management to have patience at this stage to allow the idea to develop and grow in its own way: 'If you keep picking the plant up to see if it's sending out roots it never will. But once it starts growing, this is where you become disciplined – convergent – because its progress has to be controlled.'

He is keen to emphasise the combination of divergent and convergent thinking in which divergent thinking utilises the 'interlopers' by integrating the different perspectives they bring and enabling the idea to develop and take root. By contrast, the convergent phase requires discipline and project management to monitor conformance to the check lists and standards. It is this synergistic process of divergence and convergence, Jim has observed, that delivers success time after time as long as it is being led by an individual who is really energised, enthused and determined to make it happen.

5.7 Conclusion: key lessons for building an entrepreneurial culture

Considering the experiences of Unilever, when attempting to build a more entrepreneurial culture, it can be challenging to decide where to begin. Jim returns back to the concept of leadership and management style as being crucial to establishing and nurturing the culture of the enterprise: 'Remember, ideas don't just bubble up at random, they come about because somebody at the top tells everybody else "I need your ideas and I'm going to support you to make things happen."'

He highlights that other factors such as strategy, systems and structure matter but the prerequisite for the right culture is strong leadership through clear vision and powerful people motivation.

Jim's reflection on his time at Unilever draws the conclusion that there is no precise formulation, no prescription for 'how to do it right'. Instead, his experience has led him to the conclusion that it is more like a recipe, there are success factors in common but these should be deployed to varying degrees and at different levels. Specifically he recounts the ability to recruit, motivate and utilise the diversity of creative individuals within the innovation process as paramount. He emphasises the need to create teams capable of divergent thinking, to be accepting of diversity and individuals with different backgrounds to bring different experiences, different personalities and with different expertise. Finally, he highlights the need to help to stimulate richer thinking and wider approaches to problem solving, through providing entrepreneurial freedom:

> As a manager you need to have some degree of autonomy and freedom for people to try things – scope for a bit of 'scientific dabbling' is essential. Innovation is not a defined science – it is at times more of an art. You have to try things and see what happens.

Jim reflects that structure and processes that are appropriate to the different aspects of the entrepreneurial process – supported by strong leadership, with a vision and purpose, drive and energy to make innovation happen – are essential but successful companies will, without exception, have a strategy which actually cites a specific need for innovation. If a business has a strategy with no mention of innovation then it will struggle to do so regardless of structure or process, as: 'Whenever the existing business has a little downturn where do you think the resources for new business ideas will end up?'

In answering this question, Jim reinforces that a preoccupation with the short term will mean that there will be no long term. Instead, an organisation requires an innovation strategy to set the boundaries and dedicate resources to protect the long term from the ebb and flow of the short term. Leadership and management style are critical in developing the strategy. Jim's experience of 30 years of leading innovation can be captured in six key insights that summarise the main elements to aid an organisation to build a more entrepreneurial culture:

1   Although creativity and innovation are closely linked, they are not the same.
2   There is a complex and interactive set of success factors for entrepreneurial management which must be tailored to or profiled for the company's organisation and culture.

3   Creativity can operate at all levels – individual, team and throughout the enterprise.
4   Maybe most important of all, leadership and management style are crucial for building and sustaining a company's climate for entrepreneurship.
5   Perhaps a corollary from the previous point, sustained innovation depends on the culture and climate of the organisation.
6   The key to the success for an individual innovation depends on the quality of the idea itself – it must meet real (and by definition unmet) needs for consumers, customers or society.

This final point leads us to the topic of the next chapter – different approaches for the organisation to develop better ideas.

References

1   Kuratko, D. F., Ireland, D. R. & Hornsby, J. S. (2001). 'Improving firm performance through entrepreneurial actions: Acordia's corporate entrepreneurship strategy', *Academy of Management Perspectives*, 15(4): 60–71.
2   Von Hippel, E. (1986). 'Lead users: A source of novel product concepts', *Management Science*, 32(7): 791–805.
3   Powell, T. C. (1995). 'Total quality management as competitive advantage: A review and empirical study', *Strategic Management Review*, 6 (1), pp. 15–37.
4   Burgelman, R. A. (1983). 'Corporate entrepreneurship and strategic management: Insights from a process study.' *Management Science*, 29(12): 1349– 1364.
5   Morita, A. (1992). 'S' Does Not Equal 'T' and 'T' Does Not Equal 'I'. London: The First United Kingdom Innovation Lecture.
6   Leonard, D. & Straus, S. (1997). 'Putting your company's whole brain to work', *Harvard Business Review*, 75/4 (July/August): 110.
7   Ibid.
8   Belbin, R. A. (2010), *Management Teams: Why They Succeed or Fail*. Oxford: Butterworth Heinemann, 3rd ed.
9   Tushman, M.L. & O'Reilly, C. A. (1996). 'The ambidextrous organizations: Managing evolutionary and revolutionary change', *California Management Review*, 38(4): 8–30.
10 See *A Century of Innovation: The 3M Story*: http://multimedia.3m.com/mws/media/171240O/3m-coi-book-tif.pdf.
11 Sagie, A., Zaidman, N., Michai-Hamburger, Y., Te'eni, D. & Schwartz, D. G. (2002). 'An empirical assessment of the loose–tight leadership model: Quantitative and qualitative analyses', *Journal of Organizational Behavior*, 23: 303–320.

6 Entrepreneurship with external stakeholders

Hannah Noke, Paul Kirkham and Simon Mosey

6.1 Introduction

This chapter considers where ideas for radical new products, services and business models originate. In previous chapters we have seen it requires creative individuals, but is this sufficient? It is all too easy to imagine the source of innovation as an isolated 'eureka' moment, when an inspired solution occurs to a lone inventor. In this chapter, we examine the complexity of innovation sources utilised by entrepreneurial organisations and the networks of external stakeholders that need to be mobilised as a source of novel problems in addition to a reservoir of potential solutions.

Here we propose the sources of radical innovation to be complicated and messy affairs, best conceptualised as knowledge networks. We focus first upon examples of how best an organisation can mobilise linkages across its internal network to stimulate a capability to recombine existing, albeit dispersed, knowledge. We then turn our attention to the more significant challenge of how an organisation can develop a more 'open' approach to innovation through extending its external linkages to identify unmet needs and radical new approaches. We conclude with a consideration of how to evaluate the radical potential solutions likely to emerge from such an approach.

6.2 A network approach to innovation

A common presumption is that the innovation process is a linear, parallel process, characterised by Cooper's stage gate model.[1] The beginnings of most innovations are much more complex and messy than is often presented. Research shows the actual process to be more of a spider's web, with intricate, hardly visible strands and multiple dead ends becoming detached over time.

In reality, innovation begins through connections, networks and interactive knowledge exchange both inside and outside the organisation. Only through these connections will novel insights and approaches emerge. For instance, W. L. Gore & Associates, the company best known for its breathable fabrics, acknowledge the role of networks in their development of an award-winning guitar string. Gore had no intention of entering such a highly competitive

74 *Building an Entrepreneurial Organisation*

market in which it had no experience. The opportunity emerged iteratively whilst using existing guitar strings in the test laboratory to develop a material for a better push-pull cable. John Allen, a research and development lead at Gore working on the testing, was coincidentally a keen guitarist. Together with musical colleagues across the company, he began to explore whether they could use Gore materials to produce a coated guitar string that sounded great (previously coated guitar strings had been good for preserving the life of the string but the sound quality was poor). Relying on the company's unique culture and mentoring system to support their efforts,[2] that is exactly what they did. Forming a cross-functional team they developed an exceptional guitar string coated with patented Polyweb and Nanoweb technology. They tested it with 5,000 guitar players, using players' feedback to iteratively improve the product.[3] As a result, Gore now has a strong presence as one of the best guitar string manufacturers.

Rothwell's historical examination of how organisations manage innovation provides insight into how networks have become so dominant.[4] His research categorised historical and contemporary innovation practice models and went on to predict process requirements to meet future innovation needs (see Figure 6.1). He observed the dominant innovation approach from the mid-twentieth century to be simple linear models. He categorised a transition in these models from first generation models in which innovation was initiated through technology push through to second generation models in which organisations responded to the pull of market needs. Generation one was typified by organisations developing new technologies in-house and incorporating these into new products and services to be delivered to existing customers. The process was therefore unidirectional and concentrated on pushing out internally generated ideas into the market. Towards the end of the 1950s Rothwell captured the emergence of generation two, which attempted to listen to customer preferences; a pull effect was witnessed with a consideration for the market requirements. Generations one and two were characterised by a limited external interaction restricted to the current customers of the organisation.

Figure 6.1 Summary of Rothwell's five generations of innovation process models.

Generation	Key Features
First and Second	Simple linear models – need pull, technology push
Third	Coupling model, recognising interaction between different elements and feedback loops between technology development and external customer preference
Fourth	Parallel model, integration within the firm, upstream with key suppliers and downstream with demanding and active customers, emphasis on linkages and alliances
Fifth	Systems integration and extensive networking, flexible and customised response, continuous innovation

Source: adapted from Rothwell (1994).

As time progressed during the 1960s organisations became more streamlined with a third-generation model identified as a coupled approach with interaction between internal development and external customer preferences via feedback loops. Rothwell identified significant overlap between the two, as firms sought to increase their speed to market by conducting both aspects in parallel. New external stakeholders were introduced, as upstream key suppliers were involved in the innovation process, together with the pre-existing downstream interactions with active customers. Yet the emphasis was still upon bilateral linkages and alliances. Fourth-generation processes were subsequently observed as more sophisticated variants of this approach, with organisations working with other stakeholders in the innovation process. Here the primary objective remained to increase the speed to market by reacting more quickly to customer feedback. This was achieved by increasing the frequency of feedback mechanisms and number of concurrent stages. Fifty years later these third- and fourth-generation models are commonly shared in annual reports to shareholders as 'best practice innovation process'.[5]

A fifth generation had not occurred when Rothwell's research was being conducted, but it became a prescient possibility of what was to come. Rothwell predicted innovation would become much more about systems integration and extensive networking, flexibility, customised response and continuous innovation. Rothwell's prediction is now unfolding with pioneering organisations adopting 'open innovation', through utilising networks of potential rather than existing customers alongside external inventors in the innovation process.[6] The basis of the fifth generation is the recognition that organisations do not possess all the necessary skills and resources internally for opportunity recognition or exploitation. Insightful managers acknowledge that this barrier can be overcome by building strong networks and incorporating external stakeholders in the innovation process. The following sections consider different approaches to opening the innovation process so profoundly.

6.3 Combining and recombining to find new value

We have established that contemporary innovation is complex, it is not a neat step-by-step process, and it involves many different people throughout the whole process: from external parties, suppliers and customers together with individuals across different parts of the organisation. One approach to working amongst such complexity is to revisit what the organisation already knows. Although innovation is defined as creating new value, the start point does not have to be new to the world or even new to the organisation. New value can be found, somewhat prosaically, by combining and recombining already-existing ideas. This process was characterised by Andrew Haragdon who termed it *recombinant innovation*.[7] He gave many examples where organisations took ideas from other places, industries or contexts and adapted and adopted the idea to create new value within their organisation. The quiz in Table 6.1 highlights some surprising instances of recombination creating

76 *Building an Entrepreneurial Organisation*

Table 6.1 Examples of recombinant innovation

Quiz
Question 1: Where did pasta originate? Question 2: What do you get if you combine a rubber bulb from a blood pressure monitor, an air release valve from a bike tire and an IV bag? Question 3: What was the inspiration for Henry Ford's production line?

Source: adapted from Andrew Haragdon (2003).

radical innovations of product and process; you will find the answers at the end of the chapter.

To maximise the likelihood of such recombination, organisations should encourage interaction with diverse groups of stakeholders. However, if the organisation is operating using an innovation approach where innovation is the preserve of a select few then this creates a significant barrier to change. The following section considers how to overcome such individual and organisational inertia.

6.4 How to open up innovation

Interacting with external stakeholders has been captured under the umbrella term 'open innovation', where an organisation opens the boundaries of its innovation process to others. Henry Chesborough emphasises that – because an organisation cannot employ all of the greatest people, nor can it possess all the resources, skills and capabilities required internally – the boundary for innovation should be extended to include external stakeholders in all aspects of the innovation process.[8] This is shown in Figure 6.2.[9] High-profile advocates of such an approach include Procter & Gamble, Unilever, Lego, Samsung and Peugeot.

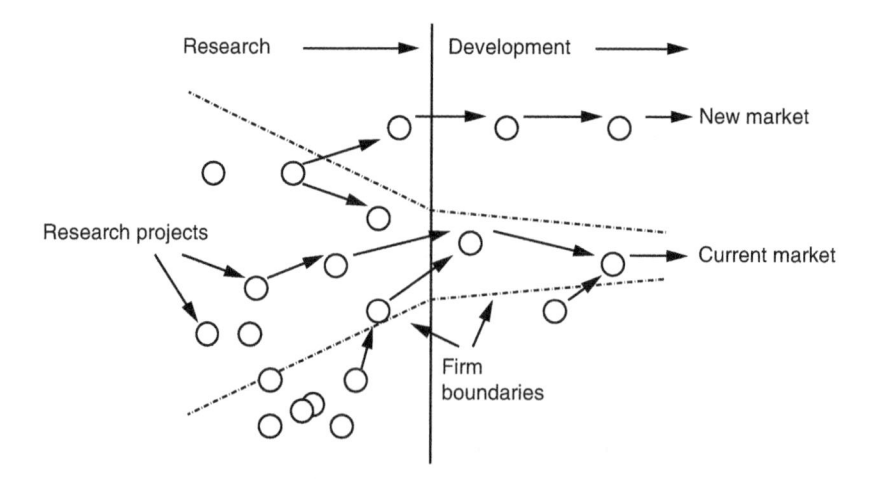

Figure 6.2 The open innovation approach.

As remarkable as this paradigm change in innovation is the propensity of organisations to share how they did so. Procter & Gamble (P&G) now report their history as being built upon open innovation, looking towards others to enable their success.[10] They proudly share examples of combining and working with others to meet a need in the market and build new capabilities more effectively. In 2000, the newly appointed CEO, A. G. Laflcy, began the transition by challenging the organisation to bring 50 per cent of its innovation from outside its boundaries.[11] Managers rose to the challenge by creating an initiative called 'Connect + Develop'. One of the first projects to be realised through Connect + Develop was the disruptive product 'SpinBrush', an electric toothbrush at a fraction of the retail price of P&G's traditional products. SpinBrush was created outside of the walls of P&G in response to an open challenge for concepts to revolutionise the dental-care market. The SpinBrush concept was one of a number of externally generated ideas and was brought into the P&G development process only after extensive prototype development and user testing. Even then SpinBrush was protected from the usual P&G bureaucracy, with three of the four original entrepreneurs joining P&G's payroll for 18 months; John Osher, the lead entrepreneur behind SpinBrush, captures his contribution succinctly: 'My job was to not allow P&G to screw it up.'[12]

Procter & Gamble managers acknowledged that such an approach was necessary to prevent the organisation from derailing such a disruptive concept. They deliberately restricted their role to the marketing and distribution of the finished product as they began the painstaking process of adjusting their internal innovation systems and procedures to be able to accommodate a more open approach.

Another high-profile advocate of the open approach is the Danish toy manufacturer Lego. In contrast to Procter & Gamble, the imperative for an open approach at Lego did not come from a challenge from their CEO. It was in response to user-led innovation. In September 1998 Lego launched an innovative new product 'Mindstorm'. In response to changing customer trends towards construction toys, developers at Lego developed a robot that could be built and programmed by the users. This led to an unexpected outcome as enthusiasts hacked the operating system behind Mindstorm, making several improvements in its functionality along the way. Lego found itself with a conundrum, to view the hacks as an infringement of its intellectual property or work with the hackers to create an ecosystem in which the game could develop and flourish. Lego chose the latter, and this has led to a series of developments in which Lego has worked with users and diverse partner organisations to expand its product range.

The evidence is growing that open innovation is an effective way to interact with external stakeholders. Yet it presents a significant management quandary in terms of specifying the scale and scope of the innovation challenge and how to evaluate the responses. Nesta advocates a ten-step approach, as highlighted in Table 6.2.[13]

Table 6.2 How to specify and evaluate an innovation challenge to external stakeholders

1 **Clear thinking**
   - Clear brief.
   - Clear notion of the business model requirements, e.g. licensing, delivery partnership, joint development.
2 **Open Competition**
   - Identify the relevant supplier, customer and consumer communities to form a competitive marketplace.
   - Use new and existing people.
   - Launch the brief.
   - Allow 2–4 weeks for entrepreneurs to respond.
3 **The Airlock**
   - Judging, developing, protecting, prototyping.
   - Use trusted agents.
4 **The Pitches**
   - Pitching
   - Feedback

Source: adapted from Nesta.

6.5 Different approaches to interacting with external stakeholders

Nesta provides a useful checklist of items; however, the utility of the approach is clearly dependent upon who you can attract to work on your challenges and your capability to evaluate radical innovation opportunities. For organisations that are, like Procter & Gamble, seeking to disrupt their current paradigm, the following two approaches can be particularly effective.

6.5.1 Look to the extremes

Traditional marketing techniques argue that to understand the customer you must engage with them; market research is essential, as it will bring certain insight into your product or service. But how useful are your existing customers when you are trying to develop radical innovations? According to Clayton Christensen, organisations are 'held captive by their customers',[14] and traditional market research techniques tell organisations what they already know. As a result, if organisations wish to find something new they need to look elsewhere.

One underutilised group are extreme users, customers who embrace using products or services in an unusual way. These users can provide invaluable insights that 'traditional' users cannot articulate. Peter Coughlan, from innovation consultancy IDEO, recounts working with a toothpaste maker: 'We wanted to look at extreme oral care users, so we found people without any teeth … At the other end of the spectrum, there was a person who had seven types of toothpaste and used them at different times of days.

It sounds extreme but yielded incredible insights about flavor, consistency, and so on.'[15]

Significant new knowledge to the organisation can be therefore be gained by tapping into users who are considered to be outside the mainstream. As Peter Coughlan from IDEO explains:

> People who fall in the middle of each user profile, the trouble is they are just a bit too average so the likes of you and I would just tell them what they have already heard, we are not going to really give them any surprises and any real insights into how we use those products or service. They tend to identify the obvious and they run with it. If you are a larger corporate conducting a lot of research you have probably heard the big universal truths about your category already so you are not finding out anything new is essentially what they are saying. It's putting how much money you would spend in the same usage year after year.[16]

OXO kitchen aids is a company built on this premise. Sam Farber, the founder, noticed that traditional kitchen gadgets were hurting his wife's hands when she used them, as she suffered from arthritis. Asking himself how the gadgets could be different and better became the inspiration for OXO. He invested time and effort talking to different groups of extreme users of kitchen gadgets, ranging from those with severe arthritis through to aspiring young chefs (under five years old in some cases!). Utilising such extreme users' insights enabled OXO to create a product with unprecedented ergonomics and functionality.

Clearly, extreme customer users can provide the inspiration for new products or services; they can also provide a rich source of ideas that can be combined with existing knowledge within the firm as suggested within the recombinant innovation section (Section 6.3). Finally, revisiting the concept of benchmarking, in which managers compare organisational processes across industries, a fruitful approach may be to seek extreme organisations from which to gain radical new process insights.

6.5.2 Crowdsourcing and online communities

Crowdsourcing, as termed by Howe (2006)[17] in *WIRED* magazine, can be defined as the process for obtaining information, products or services by enlisting contributions – either paid or unpaid – typically online. These communities are being used by organisations in different and exciting ways to solicit contributions from the outside world.

For instance, one notable success is My Starbucks Idea, which acts as a forum for exchanges around customers' experiences and opinions of their favourite coffee brand. It provides a platform in which they can engage on their own terms. The coffee giant Starbucks gains novel feedback upon the value of their customer experience and captures hitherto unarticulated perceptions from its customers. Many brands are harnessing their brand loyalty through such activities, gaining qualitatively different relationships with their customers and novel insights into their behaviour.

Other organisations are also using these communities to provide content. A pioneer in this field was the online clothing company Threadless. The company launched with the strapline: 'You are Threadless. You make the ideas, you pick what we sell, you're why we exist.'[18] Started in 2000 by Jake Nickell and Jacob DeHart as an online community for artists, it has grown rapidly through user-generated innovation. As well as being a community it is also an e-commerce site where, initially, the focus was upon user-designed T-shirts. Today it is much more. It's a place where you can purchase a canvas of your favourite work of art, order customised phone cases or invest in your favourite designs. The premise behind the organisation is that roughly 1,000 designs are submitted each week which are then shared on the company website for public vote. Seven days later the top-ten designs, based upon their popularity amongst the user community, are produced for purchase. The designers themselves are incentivised by a royalty share of their purchased designs and vouchers for Threadless, which can be converted to cash.

Crowdsourcing, which became a secondary service for Threadless, has expanded in its own right as an interactive source of investment for new ideas. Small business Shnuggle did exactly that when it launched its new baby bath product through the intermediary platform Crowdfunder (www.crowdfunder.com). Shnuggle asked for pledges of money to help get the bath to market. Potential investors were attracted by the social aspect of supporting the manufacture of the product and aiding its route to market, together with the economic aspect of receiving something in return. For a £10 investment people would receive a Shnuggle Baby Mitt; for a £25 pledge they received a Shnuggle bath as it came off the production line.[19] Kickstarter (www.kickstarter.com) provides another example of crowdfunding for entrepreneurs; the site hosts a short video promoting an idea and the community can contribute to the fledging business by pledging donations in exchange for a reward.

The ability to connect to a world of interested, like-minded people is now within the reach of many and the potential opportunity is vast – it is driving innovation into new frontiers where the boundaries of organisations, customers, funders and stakeholders are all merging. New organisations are being created within this open innovation space and existing organisations can either choose to join in or miss out at their peril.

The subsequent management challenge of evaluating such new insights and dealing with the inevitable failures is considered in Chapter 7. But first, let's consider Case 6.1.

CASE 6.1 AN EXERCISE IN PROJECT SELECTION

A fundamental aspect of innovation is choosing between possibilities. For entrepreneurs and venture capitalists, this is critical – deciding which projects offer the best prospects for a return on investment. The entrepreneurial organisation faces the same choices.

This exercise explores the difficulties associated with selecting which avenues to explore outside of the organisation's comfort zone. How are company leaders to assess widely disparate opportunities which may present themselves?

Independent entrepreneurs will use very general criteria to start with:

- Is this a real problem?
- Will anybody pay for a solution?
- In short, is this a problem worth solving?

To which they will add:

- Is there a technically feasible pathway to a solution?
- Can we protect our solution? (intellectual property – trade secret – brand)

And wider considerations:

- Is it sustainable as a business? (repeat cash sales)
- Is it scalable? (potential for growth)
- In short, is it on trend? (an expanding market? an escalating opportunity?)

The pure venture capitalist will be looking for scalability, return on investment and an exit strategy, but the entrepreneurial organisation will have other considerations depending on the nature of the organisation itself; for example, there may be a corporate social responsibility box to tick.

- Do we have any core competencies that add value to the project?
- Do we have the structure to accommodate such a project?
- In short, does it fit with our entrepreneurial vision?

Crucially, when taking a step into the unknown we need to identify the external stakeholders:

- Who are the existing players? There will be both competitors and potential partners.

- How can we engage with the consumers? There may be organisations which will welcome our interest. Who are the extreme users? Where are the niche opportunities?

Using some of these criteria and others of your own devising, complete Table 6.3 to compare the following projects.

Table 6.3 Evaluation matrix for external opportunities

Comparison Criterion	Project A	Project B	Project C	Project D	Project E	Project F

Imagine that you have a budget of 100 units of R&D resource. This is for a first round of funding. Which areas are of most interest to your organisation? All funds must be distributed but you may split the resource in whatever way you please, from equal shares to all for one. There are no 'correct' answers but you should be able to justify your conclusions.

Use the table as an advantage/disadvantage matrix. List criteria in the left-hand column and mark each project accordingly: (++) (+) (=) (−) (−−)

As examples of widely differing opportunities, we are using six issues which were chosen as the original shortlist for the Nesta 2014 Longitude Prize.[20] Nesta issued this challenge in a long tradition of offering cash prizes to encourage innovation in areas which, for various reasons, are not considered attractive market opportunities.

The six challenges that the public were invited to vote on were:

A: Dementia – how can we help people with dementia to live independently for longer?

It is estimated that 135 million people worldwide will have dementia by 2050, which will mean a greater personal and financial cost to society. With no existing cure, there is a need to find ways to support a person's dignity, physical and emotional wellbeing. The challenge is to develop intelligent, affordable integrated technologies that revolutionise care for people with dementia, enabling them to live independent lives.

B: Flight – how can we fly without damaging the environment?

If aircraft carbon emissions continue to rise they could contribute up to 15 per cent of global warming from human activities within 50 years.

This needs to be addressed in order to slow down climate change and its detrimental effects on the planet. The challenge is to design and build an aeroplane that is as close to zero carbon as possible and capable of flying from London to Edinburgh, at comparable speed to today's aircraft.

C: Food – how can we ensure everyone has nutritious, sustainable food?

One in eight people worldwide do not get enough food to live a healthy and fulfilled life. With a growing population and limited resources, providing everybody with nutritious, sustainable food is one of the biggest global problems ever faced. The challenge is to invent the next big food innovation, helping to ensure a future where everyone has enough nutritious, affordable and environmentally sustainable food.

D: Paralysis – how can we restore movement to those with paralysis?

In the UK, a person is paralysed every eight hours. Paralysis can emerge from a number of different injuries, conditions and disorders and the effects can be devastating. Every day can be demanding when mobility, bowel control, sexual function and respiration are lost or impaired. The challenge is to invent a solution that gives paralysed people close to the same freedom of movement that most of us enjoy.

E: Water – how can we ensure everyone can have access to safe and clean water?

Water is becoming an increasingly scarce resource. Forty-four per cent of the world's population and 28 per cent of the world's agriculture are in regions of the world where water is scarce. The challenge is to alleviate the growing pressure on the planet's fresh water by creating a cheap, environmentally sustainable desalination technology.

F: Antibiotics – how can we prevent the rise of resistance to antibiotics?

The development of antibiotics has added an average of 20 years to our lives, yet the rise of antimicrobial resistance is threatening to make them ineffective. This poses a significant future risk as common infections become untreatable. The challenge is to create a cost-effective, accurate, rapid, and easy-to-use test for bacterial infections that will allow health professionals worldwide to administer the right antibiotics at the right time.

Following a public vote, the Nesta Prize Committee chose antibiotics, almost certainly because of the urgency of the problem. We, however, are focusing on opportunity. Below are notes from a different response to the exercise: the discussion prompts the choice of selection criteria; the selection criteria establish the priorities; the priorities inform the final allocation of resources.

Discussion

1 *Dementia*: This is part of a wider long-term problem – aging populations. The challenge is put as technological, with no mention of prevention or cure. In an era in which tech solutions make many jobs redundant, why should we want to make caring non-human. Who will pay? This is a growing market but it's hard to see the business model.
2 *Flight*: A superficial problem in a young technology dependant on assumed growth in demand – a few whys should find it is a behavioural issue. 'To keep up with our appetite for flight' is scarcely well-defined evidence of a trend. In terms of emissions, transport in total amounts to 13 per cent, air travel even less. No technology at the moment.
3 *Food*: A tech fix for a symptom of population growth. Biggest problem – 800 million lives. Jevon's paradox – that increased efficiency might lead to increased demand. Proposed solutions such as insect protein and genetically modified (GM) food are not attractive to vegetarians and organics. Complex landscape.
4 *Paralysis*: A very specific, acute problem for a comparatively small number of sufferers (50,000 in UK) – is this one of the top six? An exoskeleton solution (e.g. prosthetics) is imitative – does it answer the real need? Technology is quite far advanced and presumably well protected.
5 *Water*: Not a problem, a thing. Too much, too little, in the wrong place – these are problems. The suggested solution is desalination – a simple problem with complex consequences. Interesting technologies like filters or fog harvesting in Chile do exist. Long history of attempted solutions from irrigation to ice harvesting.
6 *Antibiotics*: The consequence of a previous solution – a challenging problem because of difficulties of implementation – tragedy of the commons. Antibiotics have saved 80 million lives. Should not be limited to a tech solution – it is possible to imagine a mandatory solution, even a software solution (similar to livestock passports). Preventive solutions offer possibilities.

Selection criteria

It is a truism that a large return from a few can be the same as a small return from many. How can we protect our investment? How many others are in the race? Competitors or partners?

- size of market
- prospective per capita return

- possibility of alternate solutions, i.e. interesting problem area
- return sale
- defensibility of solution – can it be protected?
- blue ocean – freedom from direct competition
- technical possibility – can it be done; is there a trend in the right direction?

Table 6.4 presents one approach to external opportunity evaluation.

Table 6.4 One approach to external opportunity evaluation

	Dementia	Flight	Food	Paralysis	Water	Antibiotics
Size of the market	–	–	++	–	++	++
Profit per cap	+	–	–	+	=	–
Scalability	+	–	++	+	++	=
Alternatives	=	+	=	=	+	++
Return sales	–	+	++	–	+	++
Protection	+	+	+	+	+	+
Blue ocean	=	–	–	=	–	–
Can we do it?	+	=	=	+	+	–
	2	–1	4	2	6	3

Priorities

- Dementia – too restrictive a challenge.
- Flight – the worst opportunity; only profitable airlines are those offering the worst service!
- Food – good possibilities, very broad area, scalable.
- Paralysis – as with dementia, a very restricted market.
- Water – offers the best prospects, especially scalability.
- Antibiotics – problem not going away, therefore great opportunity for alternatives.

Allocation

So we propose the following portfolio of investment:

- Dementia – 5
- Flight – 0
- Food – 30
- Paralysis – 5
- Water – 40
- Antibiotics – 20

In this instance, it was thought that the opportunities offered by food and water outweighed the urgency of antibiotics. There are no 'correct' answers to this exercise.

6.7 Conclusion: practising entrepreneurship with external stakeholders

The purpose of this chapter has been to explore the key question:

How is entrepreneurship practised with external stakeholders?

Research has shown that innovation has evolved beyond the simple boundaries of the organisation and now involves broader communities of an organisation's suppliers and customers. External stakeholders clearly play a central role in the development of new products, services and even in creating and supporting new business models. Readers are encouraged to compare the current practices in their organisation of interest with those deployed within the case study and consider whether external stakeholders could be used to a greater extent to help define innovation challenges and propose radically innovative solutions.

The subsequent management challenge of evaluating such new insights and dealing with the inevitable failures is considered in the following chapter.

Quiz Answers

Question 1: Where does pasta originate? **China** (if you believe the legend associated with Marco Polo.)

Question 2: What do you get if you combine a rubber bulb from a blood pressure monitor, an air release valve from a bike tire and an IV bag? **The Reebok Pump Trainer**

Question 3: What was the inspiration for Henry Ford's production line? **An abattoir**

References

1. Cooper, R. (1994). 'Third-generation new product processes', *Journal of Product Innovation Management*, 11(1): 3–14.
2. See www.gore.com/en_gb/careers/associatestories/music/1234733638065.html#/all.
3. See www.elixirstrings.co.uk/support/about-us.html.
4. Rothwell, R. (1994) 'Towards the fifth-generation innovation process', *International Marketing Review*, 11(1): 7–31.
5. 2013 State of Global Innovation: New Industry Report. Imaginatek. www.imaginatek.com.
6. Lichtenthaler, E. (2011, January). 'Open innovation: past research, current debates, and future directions', *Academy of Management Perspectives*, 75–93.
7. Hargadon, A. (2003). *How Breakthroughs Happen: The Surprising Truth About How Companies Innovate*. Cambridge, Mass.: Harvard Business School Press.
8. Chesborough, H. (2003). *Open Innovation: The New Imperative for Creating and Profiting from Technology*. Cambridge, Mass.: Harvard Business School Press.
9. Adapted from www.openinnovatie.nl/open-innovatie/.
10. See www.youtube.com/watch?v=SAvwst8FAuk.

11 See https://hbr.org/2006/03/connect-and-develop-inside-procter-gambles-new-model-for-innovation.
12 See www.bloomberg.com/bw/stories/2002-08-11/why-p-and-gs-smile-is-so-bright.
13 Nesta (2010). 'Open Innovation: From marginal to mainstream'. Available at www.nesta.org.uk/sites/default/files/open_innovation.pdf.
14 See http://harvardmagazine.com/2014/07/disruptive-genius.
15 www.businessweek.com/innovate/next/archives/2008/04/ideos_extreme_customer_experiences.html (now cached).
16 Ibid.
17 Howe, J. (2006). 'The rise of crowdsourcing', *WIRED Magazine* (14.06).
18 www.threadless.com.
19 See http://shop.shnuggle.co.uk/blogs/shnugglebath/7261998-shnuggle-the-cosy-baby-bath.
20 See www.nesta.org.uk/project/longitude-prize-2014.

7 Managing uncertainty and failure

David Falzani and Paul Kirkham

7.1 Introduction

This chapter is primarily concerned with managing uncertainty and learning from failure. We draw from a series of interviews with David Falzani, based upon his unique experience of working in multinationals, such as IBM and News Corp, and fast-growing entrepreneurial organizations, one of which grew from 250 to 2,000 employees in less than two years. We first address the limits of decision making and highlight a practical approach to classify the uncertainty inherent within the majority of innovation projects. We compare and contrast the decision-making practices deployed for incremental innovations with those required for more radical projects. We draw from examples of high-technology start-ups, where the uncertainty is arguably greatest, and introduce an experimental approach to decision making used within contemporary and successful fast-growing firms. We conclude with a case study of learning from failure and highlight how such an approach can be adopted by any size of organisation.

7.2 Do you know what you don't know?

How do we know what we don't know? This is one of those questions you have to read twice.

In Chapter 1 we distinguished between external and internal imperatives for innovation and pointed out that whilst the former are inherently unpredictable, the latter are to a large extent foreseeable and in many cases inevitable; as such, they can be factored in to 'normal' business. And this highlights another distinction between external and internal imperatives, that of control. Even if the business has the agility and resilience to cope with 'unknown unknowns', it has little control over the external environment. On the other hand, with regard to internal imperatives, we ought to know what we are doing; there should not be too many surprises. And yet many businesses, large and small, fail, not as a result of something that was unforeseeable, nor as a result of something that was out of their control. With hindsight it is often blindingly obvious why they failed. A prime example is Kodak, which had to file for bankruptcy a few years ago. The company invented the digital camera that led to its demise. It wasn't wilful stupidity, so we have to ask the question: 'How did Kodak fail when it had 10,000 patents and was full of MBAs?' To help us answer that, let's take time for a little quiz (see Table 7.1).

It is called the 90 per cent confidence quiz and it is purely for fun. You are going to mark yourself. Please treat it seriously and don't search online for the answers. If you stick with it, we promise you will be surprised by the results. There are ten questions. Each question has a numerical answer so the question might be 'what is 2 plus 2?', but it is not that simple. The idea is that, for each question, you make a low estimate and a high estimate. So for every question, you have to put down two numbers; what you are trying to do is to ensure that one number is below the real answer and one number is above the real answer. For example: 'What house number in Downing Street is the prime minister's?' Set your confidence limits such that you are 90 per cent confident that the answer lies between the two numbers that you give. We could put that we are 90 per cent certain that the number in Downing Street is between 5 and 12. If we were less sure, we could make the numbers 3 and 15, or we might say we are 90 per cent confident that the numbers are between 8 and 11. It is up to you to adjust how wide the gap is until you feel 90 per cent confident.

If you get this right, expected value theory[1] says 90 per cent times 10; you should have exactly nine correct answers and one wrong – that's the score you are aiming for, nine out of ten.

This is an exercise in making judgements, making estimates. So even if you don't know the answer at all, make an estimate and make it as wide as you feel it needs to be, to be 90 per cent certain that the answer is somewhere between those numbers. You don't want to be 100% certain but you don't want to be 0% certain either.

Look at the answers as shown in Table 7.2. Count up how many you got correct; that is how many answers were within your confidence limits. You should have nine.

For us, this simple quiz is one of the most important lessons in entrepreneurial management. Think about what just happened. You are given a set of questions which you may or may not have had some inkling about. You were asked to define your own limits, a range that made you feel 90 per cent certain that you had the answer within those limits.

In business there are always high levels of unknowns, whether it is unknowns about the product, unknowns about the market, unknowns about whether people actually want that product. This is particularly so in entrepreneurial management.[2] In such situations we rely upon our judgement to make estimates and you hear words like 'gut instinct' cited to justify such decision-making approaches.

We have delivered this same quiz to MScs, MBAs, executive MBAs, PhDs, undergraduates – all highly educated people. And what we have found is that most score around three correct answers – that's 30 per cent accuracy on a test where you set your own limits!

90 Building an Entrepreneurial Organisation

Table 7.1 Questions to test your judgement

Question	Lower limit of estimate	Upper limit of estimate	Is the correct answer within limits? Y/N
How old was Martin Luther King when he died?			
What is the length of the River Nile? (miles)			
How many countries are members of OPEC?			
How many books are in the Old Testament of the King James Bible?			
What is the diameter of the moon? (miles)			
What is the weight of an empty Boeing 747? (kg)			
In what year was Mozart was born?			
What is the gestation period of an Asian elephant in days?			
What is the air distance from London to Tokyo in miles?			
What is the deepest known point in the ocean? (In feet)			

So this demonstrates two really key points:

- Human beings are dreadful at making estimates; we are naturally poor at making judgements and estimates of that type.
- Even worse, we think we are really good at it!

We will return to the implications of these profound conclusions for large organisations but for the start-up the consequences can be nasty, brutish and short.

A common perception of an entrepreneurial enterprise goes something like this:

Table 7.2 Answers to the judgement quiz

Question	Lower limit of estimate	Upper limit of estimate	Is the correct answer within limits? Y/N
How old was Martin Luther King when he died?		39	
What is the length of the River Nile? (miles)		4,258	
How many countries are current members of OPEC?		12	
How many books are in the Old Testament of the King James Bible?		39	
What is the diameter of the moon? (miles)		2,159	
What is the weight of an empty Boeing 747? (kg)		164,000–185,000 kg depending on model	
In what year was Mozart was born?		1,756	
What is the gestation period of an Asian elephant in days?		645	
What is the air distance from London to Tokyo in miles?		5,950	
What is the deepest known point in the ocean? (In feet)		36,000	

- See an opportunity.
- Build a product.
- Launch the product.

If the product is good the business will thrive. But in our experience of tech start-ups that fail, 10 per cent are technology failures but the other 90 per cent are the result of people not knowing what they don't know. In practice they lacked a sustainable business model, and the responsibility for that lies with management. I think it's true to say that the best investors in the world never invest in companies but rather invest in management. Entrepreneurial management builds that sustainable business model through managing, not ignoring, uncertainty.

7.3 Classifying uncertainty within innovation challenges

We can use a two-by-two matrix such as the one shown in Figure 7.1 to understand how different innovations call for traditional or entrepreneurial management approaches to dealing with uncertainty.

The top-right quadrant contains the 'known knowns'. This is where we'd find traditional established management processes. Motor cars, breakfast cereals, even PCs nowadays are here – improvements on existing products rather than anything new. You know what problem you are solving for customers and they know what it is that you are selling them.

By contrast, an example of the purest form of technology innovation is found in the bottom-left quadrant: this is typified within a high-tech start-up which addresses an unknown problem and an unknown solution. What that means is, basically, you have a new way to fix something but you don't really know what, because it is brand new and has never existed before. For instance, when PayPal was launched, when Microsoft created MS-DOS or when Facebook was initiated – these were completely unknown unknowns. It was highly uncertain whether people were going to ultimately derive value from them. It is such a blue sky, such an innovative and unique new offer that it's an unproven unknown solution for an as-yet-unknown problem.

Known Problem	Known Problem
Unknown Solution	Known Solution
Unknown Problem	Unknown Problem
Unknown Solution	Known Solution

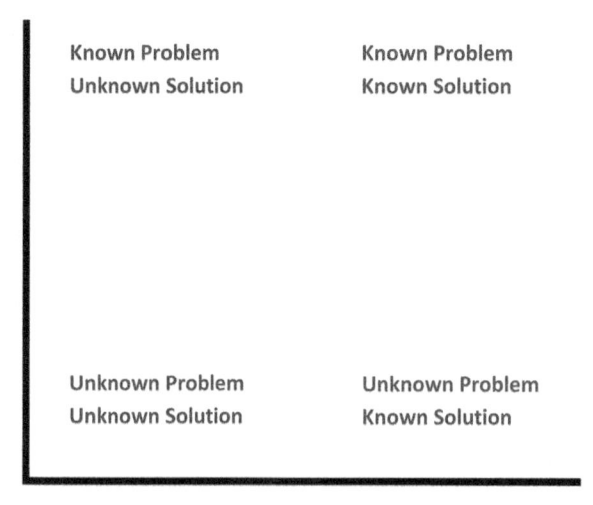

Figure 7.1 Classifying the uncertainty within potential innovation challenges for new products or services.

The top-left and bottom-right quadrants are interesting; they are a mixture of both entrepreneurial and traditional management.

Bottom right is an unknown problem but a known solution. Technology transfer is a good example of this.[3] Or entering a new market with an existing product. You know what the solution is, that is, you know your product and its track record. In fact, you know an awful lot about the product but you don't know how that new market is going to use it or accept it. There are a lot of products which work in their domestic market but, when they go to an export market, they completely fail. A simple example is that of the music industry. How many times have bands been really successful in their home country and they go to the United States and they fail or they go to Japan and they fail, or vice versa? What's happening is that the local market reinterprets what was understood to be a known offering but that market reinterprets it in a different way and sometimes that reinterpretation doesn't work.

And finally the top-left quadrant – an unknown solution but a known problem. This is a new way of doing something. Perhaps a product line extension which is building on what is already known in terms of a problem set but with an innovative solution. Before Google launched, everyone understood search engines; search engines were well established as a business model. But Google redefined the search engine; the problem set was known, what was unknown was how this new solution would fare. So this is a dynamic space – as things become known they can shift from one quadrant to another.

If we reconsider the traditional top-right quadrant, that's where conventional thinking pays off. If you are a large organisation with plenty of time and money, you might consider the traditional three-point plan: destination-based thinking[4]:

1 From current position A envisage attractive destination B.
2 Calculate back from B to A, devising a plan.
3 Execute the plan.

Such a plan will typically include validation, stage gating and prototyping before going into mass production. It works well for incremental innovations such as automotive product variants and new varieties of detergent. This approach works best when the problem and solution are known, yet is commonly advocated to be a universal approach.

We contend that for the majority of innovation challenges we need to acknowledge and manage the high levels of uncertainty. For these other three quadrants, the traditional high-risk three-step process of seeing an opportunity, building a product, and launching the product does not work! By the time you've learnt what it is that you didn't know, what it is that is preventing a successful outcome, you've gone bust.

Large corporations can spend vast amounts of money on market research and customer clinics and market analysis and still go wrong because the number of unknowns only becomes apparent post-launch.

7.4 Towards an entrepreneurial management approach

Addressing uncertainty through costly reparations following the launch of a new product might (just) be tolerable for the major players, but for smaller concerns with limited resources of time and money a different approach is needed. A lot of this is based on experience and a process to identify and develop new ideas in unpredictable places and then test them. We can sum up the differences as follows:

In-house and traditional innovation is destination based, it's hit or miss, the outcome is often unknown until it's almost complete and it requires a long-term scale and ongoing support.

By contrast, venture-led innovation has a different corporate culture. It is iterative and entrepreneurial, always fresh, always learning and with quick results – good or bad. The leading proponents of this approach have been Steve Blank and Eric Ries, founders of what has become widely known as the Lean Start-up Movement.[5]

Our take on the lean start-up is that an unsustainable business model comes about from a lack of recognition that start-ups are an experiment, as follows:

- The vision is the hypothesis.
- Validating the hypothesis is the task.
- The goal is to find a sustainable business model.
- Only when validated should it be scaled.

Validation is the task of the management team, so rather than thinking about a business plan they should think about an experiment. This is analogous to science lessons from school: you had an objective, you had a method, you had results and then you drew a conclusion. The same thing applies here – the objective is a sustainable business model. The method is finding something that people will buy that you can make money from, and only when that is validated from your results should it be scaled up.

The main elements are hypotheses and tests. We know that our destination cannot be accurately predicted. So, like scientists, we develop and test hypotheses about it and release resources only when they are confirmed.

Understanding clients and customers is therefore key, understanding what they do and what they can't do and thereby understanding their buying behaviour. We therefore advocate this experimental approach, of setting experiments in the market and actually proving or disproving a particular theory rather than relying on more traditional aspects of market research or, as we have said, making judgements or estimates ourselves. Always remember the challenge for any innovation or tech start-up is to find a sustainable business model. That is the challenge and mainly it is about sales and marketing - finding something that people will buy. Incidentally, a really useful definition of sales and marketing comes from the Chartered Institute of Marketing: it's 'the process of

Managing uncertainty and failure 95

analysing, understanding and communicating to customers and potential customers profitably'[6] and that last word 'profitably' should be the most important word to bear in mind with any new business.

Within a fast growing start-up it is typically the case that when you get new customers some sales are unsustainable. High-burden sales are the ones where you have to give a lot of information to customers before they can say to you 'Yes, I will buy it'. You either have to educate them about your product or you have to wait for their decision. So you spend an awful lot of time just bringing your customers up to speed. It might take months to educate them before they can say yes or no; if that's the case then your success rate of them saying yes had better be high enough to pay for the money you have spent in educating them. Another definition of a high-burden sale is one in which there is a very low pain incentive. It comes round to the question of how much the customer really wants the new product. If the answer is 'Really, I am not too fussed', then it is probably a high-burden sale. Here's an example: getting people to switch their bank accounts. It is said that the British are more likely to get divorced than to change their bank. The British are notoriously loyal to their bank even though they sometimes get dreadful service and poor value. People aren't really interested in changing because all bank accounts in the UK basically work. People will only swap bank accounts when they get really upset with their bank; if you offer them a much better bank account, the average customer says 'Well, I don't care really'. You can spend a lot of time and money promoting and advertising, building brand value to get that person to swap. But you have to consider your acquisition costs. Are they higher than the reward of the lifetime value of that customer? And if the customer came cheap, how long is that lifetime before they change again? So that's spending a pound to sell something that might only be worth 50 pence. Remember that word 'profitably' from the definition of sales and marketing.

The perfect customer is the evangelical customer, especially for the start-up. The cheapest and best sales force you can ever have are your customers. Evangelical customers want to tell all their friends, their colleagues, their family about your product and how great it is. It is the most effective sales force in the world, and it is free – a tremendously powerful thing to have.

For us, the single greatest validation is sales, especially repeat sales; preferably cash sales. So ideally if we have early repeat cash sales we may have something scalable.

We can use this 'creative incrementalism' to rapidly iterate business elements (model, market, offer) and create a path of small, executable steps to deploy the ideas successfully. Small executable steps provide feedback at a low cost, permitting larger investments to be made at much lower risk.

We conclude that although we are dealing with high levels of uncertainty, there are processes that can help us. David Falzani has been involved in a number of entrepreneurial businesses. He has raised about £4.5 million of venture capital in businesses that he has been personally involved with; the largest round was about £1m, but there were many smaller rounds as well; he has helped deliver pitches to investors maybe 50 times for his own businesses or for clients. Every single day he hears business ideas, many of them interesting, but the ideas themselves are of little value: it is the execution that counts.

And so, although it might surprise you, a key message he would like to get across is:

> Great entrepreneurs don't have great ideas – they have great process.

They have a process that incrementally assesses and tests opportunities, learning what the market wants and developing businesses that uncover new value.

The biggest waste in start-ups is building something nobody wants and good processes work to eliminate that error. David interprets the lean start-up movement, as proposed by Eric Ries,[7] by stating that there are three basic rules:

1. Start-ups are not mini large corporations and should not act like them.
2. Build your minimum viable product ASAP – via rapid prototyping and test marketing.
3. Test, learn, adapt and iterate – early adopters are often smarter than you are!

And there are three deadly sins:

1. 'We know what customers want.'
2. 'We can predict the future and we will act accordingly.'
3. 'We are making progress because we are advancing the plan.'

That isn't to say that you can't get lucky. It is by being in the right place at the right time that some entrepreneurs get lucky once. Naturally, it could be argued that you have to be in the game to get lucky in the first place; but it could also be argued that, over the long term, you make your own luck.

This brings us to those entrepreneurs who create wealth time and time again, often in different industries. If we acknowledge that anyone in the game can be lucky once then there must be something else that explains the track records of these serial achievers. What is their secret – and is it really a secret at all?

Our view is that entrepreneurs who succeed again and again do so because of the skills and experience they bring to bear and the processes they apply. Consistent success is built on a particular ability to solve problems, frame prospects, articulate propositions, minimise risk and maximise opportunities. And it is a truism that while good judgement comes from experience, experience comes from failure. Sometimes everything is easy and you can be successful in your venture, but when you experience failure typically you tend to learn a lot more.

To emphasise this point, David shares an example of failure being more useful than success in Case 7.1.

CASE 7.1 HOW INNOVATION REALLY WORKS: ALMOST LOSING YOUR SHIRT IN THE TAILORING BUSINESS

Back in 1998 I co-founded one of the first internet companies in Italy called Moda 1 to 1, and it is an interesting little example of how things can go well and how they can also go very badly. It started off as a business to consumer [B to C] offering. We raised about $1.5m over two rounds from a $900 million venture capital firm called the Kiwi Fund in Milan. The proposition was super-premium made-to-measure Italian suits, sold online. We had a virtual mannequin that you could scan your face on to and you could picture yourself with different suits on. We had top brands – Ermenegildo Zegna, Schofield & Smith, Loro Piana – all the top fabric brands. I wear one of these suits all the time, 15 years old and it is still going strong. So the proposition was very, very high quality Italian made suits, made to your specifications, in your body shape, ordered from the comfort of your own home and roughly 70 per cent lower in price than you would pay if you went to a tailor or a premium department store in London.

So it was a cost-saving proposition. Back then most internet businesses were based on the simple idea of saving you money. Think of Amazon when it started, the basic offer was that you could get the same books cheaper than you would in a high street bookstore. We were in the same kind of business, cost saving, as was much of the B to C market on the internet. Out of our $1.5 million we spent about $300,000 on sales and marketing. We had huge PR success – we had radio coverage, we were interviewed on television. We had over 200 press articles – all the broadsheets. The *Wall Street Journal* gave us a prize for entrepreneurship! Right up until the sales launch the business plan was executed perfectly. It was hard to get good IT people in the late 90s because there was an explosion on the demand side. So many people were building internet sites and back then you had to do it all manually, you couldn't just buy these things off the shelf like you can today. But we built the business, we did the backend, we did the database, the customer liaison, the credit card processing systems. Maybe I am biased because I was Chief Operations Officer in charge of executing that building process. Maybe we were a little bit late with some of the backend databases but believe me, we were pretty much on the ball – no problems with the tech.

So we launched – but we had no sales. We had spent $300,000 but no sales came. We had launch events in New York and London and in all kinds of cities around the world, but no sales. We thought about that and we figured 'Okay, we know what the problem is – the price is still too high' so we decided to reduce the price. We reduced the price by half and said

'Okay, stand back we are going to get hit big time – we are going to get flooded by all these people wanting made-to-measure suits'. Still no sales.

What had happened? What went wrong?

Well, hindsight is always 20/20 and from here it's very clear – fundamentally, we had made something nobody wanted. The technology all worked, the proposition seemed really good value but basically no one out there wanted what we were offering and this encapsulates the typical technology start-up mistake and it is so simple – offering something that no one wants.

From here you can see that the timing was terrible, the late 90s was the peak of the dress-down era. Even investment bankers weren't wearing suits every day and they are probably the most formally dressed business group out there. Everyone wanted to look like Steve Jobs, everyone wanted to wear polo shirts and jeans or chinos. No one was really buying suits, so it was really, really bad timing. But if we had gone to someone and said 'Would you like this top quality suit at 75 per cent off the normal price?' people would probably have said 'Yes'. The problem is you can't rely on simplistic market research. If we had gone to people and asked whether they wanted a new suit, desperately wanted a new super-premium suit right now! they would have said 'No'. If they had said to us 'Yes, I am desperate for a new suit and I would really like to have new quality suits in my wardrobe in the next year, I would really like them to be finely detailed and tailored and custom made' that would have been much better. That would have been really good market research that indicated the level of need in the market place. But we didn't have that and we should have said 'Hang on guys, we are producing something here that people aren't particularly bothered about'.

And this is a fundamental point. People were used to going to shops and feeling products and trying them on and looking in the mirror. A premium suit is a high touch product and a virtual mannequin is just not the same. There were other concerns. With mail order clothing 50 to 75 per cent returns would be quite normal and that was a bit of an issue with bespoke products because you can't put them back into stock. Actually we had found a way around that using local tailors but it really didn't matter because people weren't buying the proposition. They understood that it was much cheaper than their regular purchases but they just didn't want it.

We were asking our customers to change their buying behaviour and nowadays alarm bells go off whenever I see a business plan or a project that requires customers to do that. It's one of those things that is very hard to expect people to do unless there is a real drive to do it – unless it's something they really want.

What you have to remember is that the internet in the late 90s was the Wild West, all the way up to the 2003 economic crash. Investors were thinking what can we put money into and build very quickly. 'Don't worry about profit, just get sales. Put it into the IPO [Initial Public Offering] and make a lot of money back'. People expected 75 to 80 per cent returns per year compound on their investments. And a lot of the time it worked – a deal that Kiwi did just before us was with a company called Tiscali. So Tiscali made them I don't know how many millions. It was a land grab. When you are in that very fast-moving environment, trying to raise money, trying to execute your business plan, it is very hard sometimes just to stand back and look about and ask the right kinds of question.

We peaked at about 12 employees, the CEO set up our front office in New York City, on 5th Avenue in Manhattan – that was expensive. We had a VP of Sales & Marketing in New York – that was a couple of hundred thousand dollars in salary and healthcare benefits. It sounds like a lot of money and there came a time when we looked about and suddenly it had all gone. But we were bright people and what we had was a business plan. The plan said, this is how we spend the money. There will be a period where we have no revenue before the sales launch, the sales will start at zero and then they will gradually climb. We will still be spending money but eventually the sales will be higher than the costs and then we will make profits. That is the way any sort of business plan works – it is on a curve that starts at zero. We executed that first half very well. The problem was that the second half never happened. So, suddenly we were burning probably maybe $80,000, $100,000 a month and we didn't have any revenues. That was a very expensive cash burn rate to have and so something had to be done. We missed the B to C IPO window. The investment climate had shifted and the VC [venture capitalist] asked us to swap to a B to B [business-to-business] strategy, which we did and that eventually gave us a trade exit.

Years later with reflection – and as I said it's always 20/20 vision in hindsight – thinking about what we did wrong, in terms of execution strategy our execution was very good. I wouldn't quite say perfect but it was very good. We did the traditional business plan that said that you build up your operations and you do your product development and then you launch. The problem is that by that point you have built up a lot of cost base, you've suddenly got this big team of people, you have got a lot of cost and you are expecting to do a lot of business. But what if you are making something that no one truly wants?

The failure we made was that there was no validation through sales, and by that I mean actually getting people to prove to you that they actually want to buy this and they are willing to part with money for this product or service.

It wasn't a complete failure; we got out with our shirts intact but the remainder of the money was burnt putting the B to B operation together. And basically that was it – the whole adventure had taken around about two years.

7.6 Conclusion: managing uncertainty and failure in practice

David's experience highlights some of the differences between incremental and radical innovation. Choice is one differentiating factor in that entrepreneurs and venture capitalists can pick and choose their projects; established businesses are more constrained and therefore regress towards the incremental over time. The luxury of being at the 'right place at the right time' is not available to those of us in the 'here and now'. But the similarities in terms of failure are striking: overconfidence that we understand our customers, over-enthusiasm for our vision of the future, over-reliance on a rigid plan.

In a start-up the effects of getting it wrong are immediate and undeniable; remember, though, that three out of four types of innovation in the two-by-two matrix require entrepreneurial management and that covers most of what any organisation says it wants to do. However, let's imagine what the reaction in many a large organisation would be to a failure on the scale of Moda 1 to 1, as highlighted in Case 7.1.

In our experience, probably the project would never be spoken of again except in whispers that certain people were looking forward to new challenges.

A common pattern for large organisations, that you will hear reported on the news on a daily basis, is as follows:

First of all: denial:

- 'That's not what happened.'
- 'I would dispute those figures.'
- 'I can't comment on individual cases.'

Next: buck passing:

- 'We're going to get to the bottom of this.'
- 'Lessons will be learned.'
- 'I can't comment while the inquiry is ongoing.'

Finally: moving on:

- 'It's a very different situation these days.'
- 'It's time to draw a line.'
- 'There's no point in dwelling on the past. We need to look forward.'

Once this cycle has been repeated a couple of times the only lesson learned is to cover your back. And so the organisation succumbs to what can be called Prozac leadership,[8] typified by a pathological fear of failure disguised by relentless optimism – which brings us back to Enron and the overwhelming influence of leadership on culture.

But culture is not inevitable; whilst start-ups and established firms are very different, the most important take-aways for would-be entrepreneurial organisations are the importance of process and the fact that entrepreneurial decision-making processes can be taught and learned.

Good business might not be rocket science but entrepreneurial management offers a proven method of experiment and validation for encouraging radical innovation.

In the words of Richard Feynman, winner of the 1965 Nobel Prize in Physics: 'We are trying to prove ourselves wrong as quickly as possible, because only in that way can we find progress.'[9]

And as for relying on instinct, another scientist, Carl Sagan, when asked for his 'gut feeling', would respond: 'I try not to think with my gut.'[10]

This leads to the following question, which should help diagnose whether an organisation needs to modify its decision-making approaches to address new innovation challenges: how does the organisation manage uncertainty and failure? This is discussed further in Chapter 8.

References

1 Papoulis, A. (1984). *Probability, Random Variables, and Stochastic Processes*. New York: McGraw–Hill, pp. 139–152.
2 Stevenson, H. & Jarillo, J. C. (1990). 'A paradigm of entrepreneurship: entrepreneurial management', *Strategic Management Journal*, 11: 17–27.
3 Wright, M., Birley, S. & Mosey, S. (2004). 'Entrepreneurship and university technology transfer', *Journal of Technology Transfer*, 29(3).
4 Mintzberg, H. (2004). *Managers not MBAs: A Hard Look at the Soft Practice of Managing and Management Development*. San Francisco: Berrett-Koehler Publishers.
5 Ries, E. (2011). *The Lean Startup: How Constant Innovation Creates Radically Successful Businesses*. London: Penguin.
6 Moore, G. (1998). *Crossing the Chasm: Marketing and Selling Technology Products to Mainstream Customers*. Collins Business Essentials, New York.
7 Ries, E. (2011). *The Lean Startup: How Constant Innovation Creates Radically Successful Businesses*. London: Penguin.
8 Collinson, D. (2012). 'Prozac leadership and the limits of positive thinking', *Leadership*, 8(2): 87–107.
9 Feynman, R. P. (1992). *The Character of Physical Law*. London, Penguin UK. This was part of a series of classic lectures, delivered in 1960 and recorded for the BBC.
10 Sagan, C. (1987). 'The Burden of Skepticism', *Skeptical Inquirer*, 12.

8 Building an ambidextrous organisation

Hannah Noke and Simon Mosey

8.1 Introduction

This chapter considers the challenge of capturing new knowledge and transforming that knowledge into new products, services or ways of working. We consider the need for different approaches to capture and share new information when compared to those required for new 'know how'. We explore how organisations can build a capability to absorb new knowledge from external partners and customers and the dilemmas that this can create. One of the most pertinent challenges is how an organisation can reconcile the need to learn how to improve current practices with developing the capability to recognise and exploit new opportunities. We conclude that successful organisations encourage and support an ambidextrous approach. Here employees are encouraged by a supportive culture and reward structure to pursue a learning approach that is appropriate to the innovation challenge that they face.

8.2 Capturing tacit and explicit knowledge

As a foundation for innovation, capturing the right knowledge enables organisations to gain a powerful competitive advantage. Yet managing knowledge creation and exchange is one of the most significant challenges for leaders of organisations. If an organisation could harness even a fraction of the total knowledge of its employees, it would easily outperform its rivals.

Capturing knowledge is challenging, as different approaches are required for different types of knowledge. Fundamentally different practices are necessary to capture *explicit knowledge or information,* and *tacit knowledge or know-how* respectively.[1] Explicit knowledge or information is composed of data, raw observations that have been categorised, interpreted and contextualised to provide order. Explicit knowledge is therefore information that is easily codifiable, that can be transmitted from one individual to another without it losing its meaning. Examples may include company handbooks, textbooks and how-to-videos, all containing facts that can be easily exchanged.

By contrast, tacit knowledge, or know-how, involves knowledge that is difficult to codify, complex in nature and therefore challenging to exchange with others through written or verbal communication. Language is often cited as an example of tacit knowledge as the rules of a language are difficult to write down and articulate. To learn a language with all its nuances requires practical immersion in addition to theoretical instruction. The properties of know-how suggest that, when compared to information, appropriate know-how is more likely to result in competitive advantages that are sustainable because the very properties that make exchange difficult also constrain imitation by rivals.[2] The critical aspect for entrepreneurial organisations is how tacit knowledge is created and exchanged to enable opportunity identification and exploitation.[3]

As we saw in Chapter 2, the recognition that tacit knowledge could also be found at a group level invites organisations to consider knowledge in an aggregated way in the form, for example, of core competencies or dynamic capabilities.[4] We propose that organizations should therefore pay attention to the role that different groups play in the creation, management and transfer of the firm's knowledge. For instance, at the operational level an understanding of which groups possess the key entrepreneurial knowledge of the organisation, and how different groups transfer and share knowledge, is critical. Similarly, at the managerial level one must consider who is responsible for constantly monitoring this knowledge flux to see possibilities to improve process, product or services and to identify potential business opportunities; these are pertinent questions that arise from the idea that tacit knowledge is present also at a group level. This resonates with empirical work considering the insights gained by boundary spanners, individuals who identify opportunities between groups by working closely with groups in disparate domains and over a sustained period of time.[5]

An empirical example of such an effective group-learning approach, within a large organisation, was observed by Dyer and Nobeoka.[6] They captured the different approaches that Toyota used for different types of knowledge and they argued that managers had to be cognisant of which approach should be used for which type of knowledge: '[Managers should] allow for a "matching" of the type of knowledge with a process that is the most effective and efficient at transferring that particular type of knowledge'.

As highlighted in Figure 8.1, for explicit knowledge exchange Toyota made use of meetings with suppliers and supplier associations. Alternatively, for tacit knowledge exchange the company utilised employee transfers, problem solving teams and voluntary learning teams.

8.3 Organisational learning as part of the innovation process

Knowledge capture is clearly important, but to leverage this knowledge an organisation also needs to formalise organisational learning. Here, an effective first step can be to introduce learning as a feedback mechanism at the end of the innovation process. Typically, such learning can be formally embedded

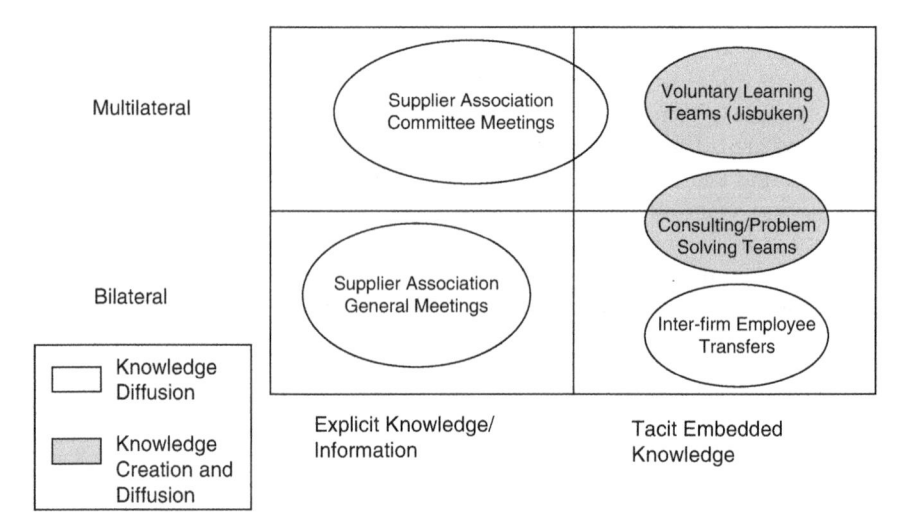

104 Building an Entrepreneurial Organisation

Figure 8.1 Knowledge transfer practices at Toyota.
Source: adapted from Dyer and Nobeoka (2000).

upon completion of an innovation project. For instance, when the product or service has been launched, a review mechanism can be introduced to improve future performance.

In addition to reviews and exchanges, another effective practice is building stores of knowledge that can subsequently be called upon as sources of innovation. As we saw in Chapter 6, interacting with external stakeholders to better understand their problems and potential solutions for those problems, if captured effectively, can be a valuable source of radical innovation.

For example, Miele, the German domestic-appliances manufacturer, has been storing knowledge about allergen elimination for more than 75 years in researching, developing and testing its award-winning vacuum cleaners. This has been achieved through 'Listen and Watch' teams who actively participate in ethnographic research, that is, observation and questioning potential customers to understand their cleaning behaviour. As a result, new Miele vacuum cleaners were developed with a twelve-stage filtration system for unprecedented performance in allergen removal from carpets. These products would never have been conceived without an in-depth knowledge of allergy sufferers' lives. Observing how allergy suffers approached vacuuming provided invaluable insights, such as seeing them vacuum the same piece of carpet or mattress numerous times. When questioned why they were doing this, the answer was 'to make sure it is clean'. This knowledge was also used to develop a traffic-light system on the vacuum head highlighting when the area was free from allergens – thereby ensuring confidence for the allergy sufferer.

In sum, learning should be embedded throughout the entire innovation process. Google is one example of such embedded learning as it has effectively reused past experience to improve future innovations (see the article by P. Williams, cited previously). To address an innovation challenge of understanding the evolving social media space, Google launched a number of services such as Google Buzz and Orkut, which were not adopted by customers as anticipated. These launches did, however, provide four years of valuable knowledge that drove a shift in strategy when, in 2011, founders Brin and Page decided upon an ambitious 100-day launch of a new social media service, Google+. Google+ gained frantic press coverage at launch but did not deliver on its objective, which was to replace Facebook's product. Despite the lukewarm reception by customers, this project provided a greater level of knowledge of how to provide identity services across products, a growing competitive space that Google has subsequently capitalised upon. As we saw in Chapter 7, mistakes or failures can provide knowledge that can be drawn upon and learnt from to develop further innovations.

8.4 Learning from others

Learning does not have to be a solitary activity restricted to the boundaries of the organisation. Learning is often most powerful when it reaches outside the organisation, by learning from others. Alliances, working in partnerships or as a collective group working towards a shared goal, are just some of the ways organisations learn from each other. When is it appropriate for an organisation to learn from others? It is often a response to understanding that there might be a lucrative market opportunity that an organisation does not have the necessary capabilities to exploit alone.

Ericsson, the Swedish telecoms equipment maker, and Sony, the Japanese electronics company, had such an understanding when they merged their mobile phone handset businesses in 2001 to create Sony Ericsson Mobile Communications, a 50–50 joint venture. Ericsson had struggled to exploit the growing handset market in which their products were considered functional yet aesthetically undesirable by customers. By contrast, Sony had not managed to gain significant market share in Europe as the functionality of its handsets was considered outdated despite attractive designs. Together, the two companies had a much stronger chance of building on their individual capabilities, and they went on to develop a series of award-winning new camera phones for the European market.

Learning from others can come in many different guises. Benchmarking across different industries can bring mutually beneficial learning experiences. In 2008 Procter & Gamble (P&G) and Google started a project in which they exchanged employees for a few weeks at a time to learn from each other. The intention for P&G was to expose brand managers to the realisation that people were spending less time watching TV and more time online. It was thought that direct exposure to employees at Google's headquarters would be an effective way for them to experience this changing cultural phenomenon. Likewise, Google was interested in learning more about how to build brands, an area that P&G was renowned for. The learning proved to be mutually beneficial as the companies were not in direct competition for customers.

This approach can also be effective within firms, especially large multinationals. Toyota's approach is to take between 200 and 300 new recruits before they are employed in a new factory and set them to work in an existing factory; there they learn from experienced assembly line workers for several months. Following this training period, the newly trained employees are placed back in the new factory, alongside 100–200 long-term, highly experienced Toyota workers to ensure Toyota's finely tuned production process is fully transferred. This method of learning demonstrates another way that Toyota encourages the sharing of tacit knowledge, in addition to those approaches visited at the beginning of this chapter.

8.5 Building an organisational capability to absorb new knowledge

The creation of 'new' knowledge, understanding and intelligence informs entrepreneurial and competitive behaviour. Cohen and Levinthal[7] first coined the term 'absorptive capacity', defining it as 'the firm's ability to identify, assimilate and exploit knowledge from the environment'. Viewed as a dynamic capability, it is an embedded process that can enable change and evolution, vital for innovation to take place, 'these capabilities enable the firm to reconfigure its resource base and adapt to changing market conditions in order to achieve a competitive advantage'.[8] It is essentially the ability of the organisation itself to learn and, as with most things, the more you practise the proficient you become.

According to Zahra and George, and as seen in Figure 8.2, the process of absorptive capacity can be broken down into two subsets of potential and realised capacity; potential absorptive capacity enables the firm to be receptive

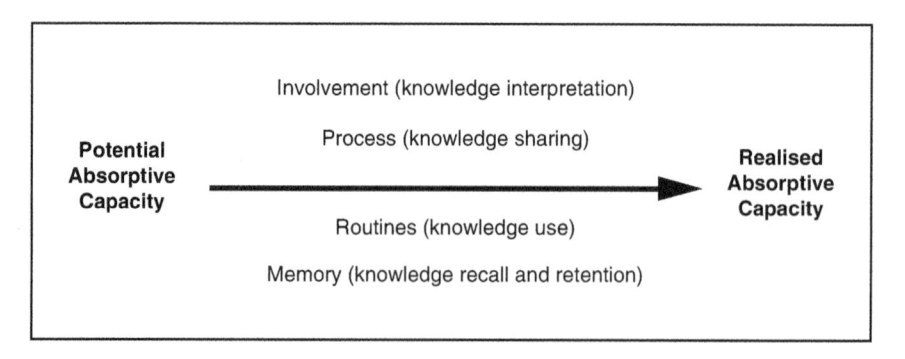

Figure 8.2 Absorptive capacity.
Source: adapted from Zahra and George (2002).

to acquiring and assimilating external knowledge. Acquisition is defined by Lane and Lubatkin[9] as being the capacity to recognise, understand the importance of and acquire the external knowledge needed for the organisation to operate. From an innovation viewpoint it can be seen as a motivator for seeking out new trends and information to be used to stimulate innovation. The second part of potential absorptive capacity refers to the capacity of the firm to integrate external knowledge through routines and processes that enable understanding to take place as well as the ability to analyse, process and interpret the information obtained from external sources.[10]

This can be illustrated in the early development of the video company Netflix. Here, managers demonstrated potential absorptive capacity through recognising the opportunity inherent in changing customer preferences for video-streaming services when compared to DVD rentals. CEO Reed Hastings challenged managers to process, interpret and react to the changing trend. Managers responded and began to utilise profits from their existing DVD rental business to help build a faster-growing but lower margin business providing video streaming. Managers thereby exhibited realised absorptive capacity by enabling a transition from one platform to another and eventually cannibalised their core business ahead of their rivals.

Realised absorptive capacity involves two elements of the process by which the organisation transforms the external information that it has gathered; *transformation* refers to the capability of the firm to develop and refine the routines that facilitate combining existing knowledge and the newly acquired and assimilated knowledge. It is worth noting here that the transformation of knowledge can be achieved through adding to existing knowledge, suppressing what is already known or even reinterpreting existing knowledge based on new information[11] In addition to transforming knowledge, realised absorptive capacity involves action, which involves the firm's capacity to utilise the new external knowledge competitively in order to enable it to achieve its strategic goals.[12] This element requires routines to be created in order for firms to refine, extend and leverage its existing competencies, or even develop new ones to take account of the newly acquired and transformed knowledge.

Absorptive capacity is essentially driven by past/prior knowledge and experience and the routines they form.[13] It goes some way to explaining why some larger firms often lack a willingness and ability to cannibalise existing products/services[14] to pursue radical change. Because the embedded routines can prevent learning and acquiring, assimilating, transforming and exploiting new knowledge destabilizes the status quo. For younger firms, Chandy and Tellis[15] claim that the lack of such past/prior knowledge in young firms gives them a 'learning advantage of newness' versus old/established firms.

This dichotomy can be conceptualised as two different types of learning that impact the outcome for innovation – exploitative learning and explorative learning – and that typically result in qualitatively different innovation outcomes.

Exploitative learning is a directed search emphasising limited variety. Its activities include refinement, choice, production, efficiency, selection, implementation and execution.[16] Exploitative search is done by pursuing knowledge that is closely related to the organisation's pre-existing knowledge bases; the knowledge acquired is established and carries a known certain and immediate outcome, typically in the form of incremental innovations.

Explorative learning activities include search, variation, risk taking, experimentation, play, flexibility, discovery or innovation.[17] Knowledge generated by such activities is often distant from the existing knowledge base of the organisation; the knowledge created is highly uncertain in terms of its value to the firm and may prove valuable after time in the form of radical innovations.

8.6 Managing exploitative and explorative learning: being ambidextrous

One of the key questions is how does an organisation sustain both types of learning in order to be able to fuel innovation, especially when legacy effects tend to encourage simple exploitation (see March[18]). Exploitative learning is necessary to be able to efficiently and effectively manage the requirements for today through most effectively exploiting what the organisation already has. Yet if the organisation is to be responsive and remain competitive, it must seek to be adaptive to changes in the external environment by exploring new alternatives. A clear tension exists between the two types as they compete for scarce resources – seeking a balance is one dilemma of how to manage innovation.

The literature argues that one way for organisations to manage the duality of exploitation and exploration is through being ambidextrous. The issue is that both types of learning are governed by different approaches, resources, processes and selection criteria; these are often at conflict, creating tensions in the organisation. March reasoned that organisations can encourage and manage this process of exploitation and exploration through creating different organisational structures and strategies that support the aims being sought – referred to as structural ambidexterity.[19] Here the structure for managing exploitation and exploration activities run parallel to one another and are therefore kept separate.

Of the two types of innovation, organisations frequently find radical innovation the most difficult; the exploration of new areas in which to develop products and services or even rewrite the existing business model is understandably daunting. Organisations find exploiting what they already have to be more straightforward and easier to justify using legacy performance measures. However, by its very nature radical innovation requires a different way of thinking that can be very different to the 'usual way of working'. It is for this very reason that advocates of structural ambidexterity argue its usefulness – exploration requires different support mechanisms to exploitation, the selection criteria should be different, as should the development process. If the traditional, exploitative criteria were applied, then it would likely halt or even 'kill' radically different projects. By creating an organisational structure that supports the two different approaches, the two can co-exist and the organisation can seek to gain a competitive advantage by continuing to improve for today whilst concurrently building an organisation for tomorrow.

8.7 It is more than just structure

A common approach to addressing the challenge of ambidexterity is to isolate the two types of learning within separate parts of the organisation. The sole responsibility for explorative learning is placed within a research and development unit and the responsibility for exploitative learning is placed within functional or product/market business units. Whilst such separation seems appealing due to its simplicity, the end result is a lack of interaction between the respective units. Due to fundamental differences in the methods used to capture, evaluate and deploy new knowledge, a breakdown in communication will occur and consequently innovation performance will decline over time.[20] Birkinshaw and Gibson advocate an alternative strategy – contextual ambidexterity – in which each individual employee makes a choice between the two learning approaches in the context of their everyday activities.[21] They observe successful organisations such as Intel, Hewlett-Packard and 3M managing the need for exploitation and exploration in this way.[22]

Birkinshaw and Gibson propose the following four attributes to be necessary for employees to be able to work in such a contextual ambidextrous way[23]:

- Ambidextrous individuals take the initiative and are alert to opportunities beyond the confines of their own jobs.
- Ambidextrous individuals are cooperative and seek out opportunities to combine their efforts with others.
- Ambidextrous individuals are brokers, always looking to build internal linkages.
- Ambidextrous individuals are multitaskers who are comfortable wearing more than one hat.

The four attributes must be present within the ambidextrous individual. However, enabling an individual to be ambidextrous in this way requires a facilitative organisational context. A capacity for exploitation and exploration needs to be present in both the organisation and the individual. At an organisational level, 'contextual ambidexterity can be defined as the collective orientation of the employees toward the simultaneous pursuit of alignment and adaptability'.[24] In order for individuals to exhibit such behaviours, support structures and culture are crucial, enabling the contextual individual to be able to act outside of the confines of the role, acting in the broader interests of the organisation. It therefore requires coherence among the practices supporting culture, leadership and strategy to enable individuals to act in this way. The organisation must have clear support mechanisms that reward exploitative and explorative learning and an entrepreneurial strategy that emphasises the need for incremental and radical innovation.

8.8 Conclusion: Reconciling different learning approaches

This chapter has illustrated the importance of knowledge and learning to an organisation in creating incremental and radical innovations. We emphasise that very different approaches are necessary for different types of knowledge and sustained management attention is necessary to sustain exploratory learning because exploitative work is easier to justify and measure. Within this chapter we illustrated that the process by which an organisation learns is linked to the structures, processes and cultural practices explained in earlier chapters. If such practices are aligned and coherent, this will encourage all employees to recognise which types of learning are required for which type of innovation challenge and deploy those practices accordingly. This leads to the final diagnostic question:

> How does the organisation reconcile exploitative and explorative learning?

Case 8.1 considers two highly creative organisations, Disney and Pixar, that have changed their learning practices over time. Disney has a prestigious history of exploratory learning, enabling the firm to conquer markets from theme parks to computer games, yet we see their learning processes became more exploitative over time and the firm consequently becoming less competitive within their home market of animated movies. Pixar, in turn, won numerous awards and achieved unprecedented box office success for a series of computer-animated films, each pioneering new animation, computation and filming technologies. Disney leaders therefore facilitated a merger with Pixar to revitalise the learning capabilities of Disney animation; we examine the resulting reconciliation of very different learning practices and how they proved to be a very powerful stimulus to innovation.

CASE 8.1 RECONCILING LEARNING PRACTICES AT DISNEY AND PIXAR

A quick question: who was responsible for first full-length animated feature film?

Many people will answer Walt Disney in 1937 with *Snow White and the Seven Dwarfs*. And yet the earliest surviving example is a bit older: Lotte Reiniger's *Die Abenteuer des Prinzen Achmed* (The Adventures of Prince Achmed) a colour-tinted silhouette animation premiered in 1926 to great acclaim from the likes of Jean Renoir, Fritz Lang and Bertholt Brecht. (A restored version can be found on YouTube.) It was the year before the first 'talkie' *The Jazz Singer* changed everything. Walt Disney was working on short black-and-white cartoons in his new studios. His early films (also accessible on YouTube) do not compare that well with

Reiniger's in terms of artistry or ambition and yet it is Disney who is remembered. Why?

With the considerable proviso that Reiniger was a woman, rendered effectively stateless when she left Nazi Germany in 1933, there are fundamental differences between her and Disney. Essentially, Reiniger's talent lay in her two hands; Walt Disney (ably backed by his less visible brother, Roy) built a scalable system. Following her breakthrough product, Reiniger did not innovate significantly – doing better but not doing differently: in Schumpeterian terms, her response to change was more reactive than creative.[25] On the other hand, Disney embraced and pioneered developments in all of Tidd and Bessant's four Ps.[26] Here are a few:

- *Products*: a long list of characters from Mickey Mouse onwards, all with extremely profitable merchandising.
- *Processes*: cel animation; synchronised sound; digital recording.
- *Position*: Disneyland theme parks, *Fantasia* animated musical, Disney television channel for children.
- *Paradigm*: the 'whole product' – starting with *Who's Afraid of the Big Bad Wolf?*, a hit song tied in to the film *Three Little Pigs*. But as Walt is reputed to have said, 'you can't top pigs with pigs'; Disney moved on in a way that Reiniger, despite her huge talent, did not.

Fast forward to the turn of this century and another burgeoning new technology: computer-generated imagery (CGI). While it is true that Disney acted as distributors for the first CGI-animated feature *Toy Story*, for once the company was behind the curve as regards the creative process. Anecdotally, the moment that Disney decided to 'innovate by acquisition' was when a senior executive noticed that none of the figures in a parade at Disneyland that were less than ten years old were Disney's own home-grown characters. The merger between Disney and Pixar, the CGI pioneers, is a story well known and told by the various players, but we will concentrate on the organisational learning aspect that made Pixar so successful in the first place.

Pixar is a prime example of the new way of doing things that we described in Chapter 1 – flexible and fast moving, with each new movie breaking new ground in terms of animation-technology development and deployment. It is worth revisiting the movies in order of their release date to observe the radical changes in visualisation as the computer-generated worlds appear more and more authentic and compelling.

Following the merger an immediate tension was observed between Pixar and Disney's strategies for line extensions. Prior to the merger Pixar had a policy of 'no movie sequels.' Following the merger, Disney managers proposed that Pixar should utilise their exploitative-learning approach.

A sequel to *Toy Story* was to be produced as a direct-to-video project with commensurate lower costs and quality. Pixar managers disagreed and a compromise was hammered out following a great deal of debate. Pixar would produce a sequel but it would still incorporate radical new features which they argued was a central characteristic of their previous successes. Despite the fact that Pixar animators were already working on another groundbreaking movie, *A Bug's Life*, they pioneered new technologies and approaches within *Toy Story 2*. One example was the use of 'dust' in an animated movie for the first time, which required novel computational and animation approaches to be assimilated and adopted, a costly and time consuming endeavour. Throughout the process, Pixar managers insisted on retaining one quality standard for the studio: 'a loud statement ... that it was unacceptable to produce some good films and some mediocre films.'[27]

To their credit, Disney recognised this and gave them free rein.

Pixar's rationale for maintaining their pioneering approach is explained by one of the founders and the current president of Walt Disney and Pixar Animation Studios Ed Catmull[28]:

> We as executives have to resist our natural tendency to avoid or minimize risks, which, of course, is easier said than done. In the movie business and plenty of others, this instinct leads executives to choose to copy successes rather than try to create something new. That's why you see so many movies that are so much alike. It also explains why a lot of films aren't very good. If you want to be original, you have to accept the uncertainty, even when it's uncomfortable, and have the capability to recover when your organization takes a big risk and fails.[29]

The learning approaches that Pixar employ are a key driver of its pioneering performance. Animation does differ from other businesses, even other film making and indeed theatre productions in one respect: you can't send a show out on the road as a preview, neither can you improvise, ad lib or rewrite the script on the set. In the animation business, the lean start-up is not an option, you have to learn as you go, before the project is finished. One way Pixar does this is with a 'Brain Trust' that reviews work in progress. This is crucially different from an exploitative learning stage gate process. Here senior managers have a checklist of performance criteria based upon previous successful projects; the project is compared to this checklist and if it falls short the project has to repeat the previous stage or be stopped. By contrast, Pixar's Brain Trust has no authority to stop the project or predetermined 'success criteria'. The company argues that this encourages new film directors to seek unvarnished expert opinion which they can take or leave in a spirit of mutual trust and respect.

This peer culture is also apparent in the review procedure *after* a project is finished. But it isn't easy; everyone wants to move on. As Catmull says of post mortems: 'Everyone learns but nobody likes them. People in general want to talk about what went right rather than what went wrong.' One technique is to ask for a list of the five things film makers would do again along with the five things they wouldn't. 'The balance between the positive and the negative helps make it a safer environment.' This bears comparison with the supportive peer-review system widely used in education with the acronyms WWW and EBI (What Went Well and Even Better If). Perhaps surprisingly, Pixar's seemingly explorative post-mortems also rely on large amounts of data. As Catmull explains:

> Because we are a creative organisation, people tend to assume that that much of what we do can't be measured or analysed. That's wrong. Most of our processes involve activities and deliverables that can be quantified. We keep track of the rates at which things happen, how often something has to be reworked, whether a piece of work was completely refinished or not and when it was sent to another department. Data can show things in a neutral way, which can stimulate discussion and challenge assumptions arising from personal impressions.[30]

Such a balance of peer review without predetermined performance measures and alongside data analysis with rigorous efficiency metrics illustrates how Pixar manages to conduct both types of learning systematically after each innovation project – ambidexterity in practice.
Nevertheless, Catmull recognises that this requires significant management effort to maintain: 'Left to their own devices, people will game the system to avoid confronting the unpleasant.' So they have to vary the format, and that exemplifies the company – fast moving and flexible, but underlain by a set of principles and practices that embeds learning at all levels. And this is modelled by the leadership who insist: 'It must be safe to tell the truth.'[31]

References

1 Grant, R. M. (1996). 'Prospering in dynamically-competitive environments: Organizational capability as knowledge integration', *Organization Science*, 7(4): 375–387.
2 Nonaka, I. & Takeuchi, H. (1995). *The Knowledge Creating Company: How Japanese Companies Create the Dynamics of Innovation*. New York: Oxford University Press.
3 Munoz, C., Mosey, S. & Binks, M. (2013). 'The tacit mystery: Reconciling different approaches to tacit knowledge', *Knowledge Management Research and Practice*, 1–10.
4 Grant, R. M. (1996). 'Prospering in dynamically-competitive environments: Organizational capability as knowledge integration', *Organization Science*, 7(4): 375–387.

5 Williams, P. (2002). 'The competent boundary spanner', *Public Administration*, 80(1): 103–124.
6 Dyer, J. H. & Nobeoka, K. (2000). 'Creating and managing a knowledge-sharing network: The Toyota case', *Strategic Management Journal*, 21: 346.
7 Cohen, W. A. & Levinthal, D. A. (1990). 'Absorptive capacity: A new perspective on learning and innovation', *Administrative Science Quarterly*, 35(1): 128–152.
8 Zahra, S. A. & George, G. (2002). 'Absorptive capacity: A review, reconceptualization and extension', *Academy of Management Review*, 27(2): 185–203.
9 Lane, P. J. & Lubatkin, M. (1998). 'Relative absorptive capacity and interorganizational learning', *Strategic Management Journal*, 19(5): 461–477.
10 Zahra, S. A. & George, G. (2002). 'Absorptive capacity: A review, reconceptualization and extension', *Academy of Management Review*, 27(2): 185–203.
11 Ibid.
12 Lane, P. J. & Lubatkin, M. (1998). 'Relative absorptive capacity and interorganizational learning', *Strategic Management Journal*, 19(5): 461–477.
13 Levinthal, D. A. & March, J. G. (1993). 'The myopia of learning', *Strategic Management Journal*, 14(8): 95–112.
14 Chandy, R. K. & Tellis, G. J. (2000). 'The incumbent's curse? Incumbency, size and radical product innovation', *Journal of Marketing*, 64(3): 1–17.
15 Ibid.
16 March, J. G. (1991). 'Exploration and exploitation in organizational learning', *Organization Science*, 2(1): 71–87.
17 Ibid.
18 Ibid.
19 Ibid.
20 Gibson, C. B. & Birkinshaw, J. (2004). 'The antecedents, consequences, and mediating role of organizational ambidexterity', *Academy of Management Journal*, 47: 209–226.
21 Ibid.
22 Ibid.
23 Ibid.
24 Birkinshaw, J. & Gibson, C. (2004). 'Building ambidexterity into an organization', *Sloan Management Review*, 45: 47–55.
25 Schumpeter, J. A. (1934). *The Theory of Economic Development*. New Brunswick, NJ: Transaction Publishers.
26 Tidd, J. & Bessant, J. (2011). *Managing Innovation: Integrating Technological, Market and Organizational Change*. Hoboken, NJ: Wiley.
27 Catmull, E. (2014). *Creativity Inc: Overcoming the Unseen Forces that Stand in the Way of True Inspiration*. London, UK: Bantam Press, p. 64.
28 Ibid. (All quotations from Ed Catmull in this section come from this source.)
29 Ibid., p. 109.
30 Ibid., p. 191.
31 Ibid., p. 225.

9 Diagnosing an entrepreneurial change programme

Simon Mosey and Paul Kirkham

9.1 Introduction

This chapter provides an integrated model for building an entrepreneurial organisation. We introduce an analytic framework that can be used initially to capture the current entrepreneurial practices within an organisation and diagnose any shortfall between those practices and desired innovative outcomes. It then presents a range of possible approaches that can be considered to address those shortfalls. Case studies are provided to highlight how different deficiencies in practice can be addressed within the private and public sector and across industries from circuses to aerospace. We explain how these diverse organisations identified and adopted new and more appropriate practices through an entrepreneurial change programme that transformed behaviour. We conclude with an overview of how one industrial and consumer products company, 3M, has systematically revolutionised all of its practices to provide sustained innovative performance.

9.2 A case-based diagnostic approach

In Chapter 1 we argued that case-based reasoning was the most appropriate decision-making tool for managers seeking entrepreneurial change.[1] In this chapter we break this down into a simple three-stage approach. First, managers should 'diagnose' which entrepreneurial practices need to change for the organisation to meet its innovation goals. Then, managers should explore how they can change their practices through considering what they could improve, simplify or do differently. Here an exploration of how other organisations changed their practices can be a useful start point. Finally, an action plan has to be agreed upon detailing how these practices can be translated so that they will be effective within the new organisational context and prescribing who is best placed to effect such a change. This is illustrated through the following case of an opportunity-led innovation that occurred through such a systematic approach (Case 9.1).

CASE 9.1 AN EXAMPLE OF OPPORTUNITY-DRIVEN ENTREPRENEURSHIP: PUREGYM

Leisure entrepreneur Peter Roberts founded PureGym in 2009 with four sites in Leeds, Manchester, Wolverhampton and Edinburgh. It has expanded rapidly; although plans for a stock market flotation in 2016 were put on hold, there is no lack of confidence that the company will continue to grow.[2]

What is being done differently? The established model in Britain has been at the high end – saunas, swimming pools, racquet courts, personal trainers – with the archetype being David Lloyd Leisure. Many of us are familiar with the business model associated with gyms and leisure centres like this; annual subscriptions are sold in January, and heaven forbid that all of these are fully utilised. PureGym operates at the other end of the market. As the name suggests, it's just a gym, open 24 hours a day, typically with two staff, supported by a dozen self-employed trainers. So that is the new product/service. The new process is a monthly subscription – easy to join but also easy to leave, although the company claims to have a rejoining rate of 35 per cent. The new position is in a new market; apart from the undoubtedly significant price and convenience, low-cost gyms are not in direct competition with the high-end ones. If we look for where the value lies the essential question remains 'Is it an upgrade and from what?' The answer is probably home gym equipment – the exercise bike in the spare room, the cross-trainer in the garage – and who really has the space for all these?

Note that, like many an entrepreneur from Henry Ford onwards, Peter Roberts did not invent anything new. He spotted a proven trend towards low-cost gyms in the United States, Germany and Scandinavia and put it together with a subscription model more in tune with a mobile phone than a membership card. What was so attractive?

As he told *The Telegraph*, 'Having been in hotels and pubs where cash and big staff numbers were an interesting challenge, going into a business with relatively low staff numbers and no great need for cash sounded pretty attractive.'[3] Low-cost gyms are cash generative and so, unlike many high-growth businesses, cash flow is not an overriding concern.

If we look at the trends that this innovation fits, there is the obvious one towards personal fitness, but this is against a background of what some call the totally integrated consumer who conducts most of his or her transactions via a smart phone. And of course PureGym is perfectly in line with the re-invention of the High Street

PureGym has had to innovate as it has grown – for example, there has been a shift from repurposing existing properties towards new-builds.

Challenges for the future include operating within changing regulatory frameworks; acquisitions and mergers may attract the interest of the UK Competition and Markets Authority. By 2016, however, the company had become the largest UK operator in the sector, with nearly 170 gyms and approximately 820,000 members.

We can see many of the key issues highlighted in previous chapters in the case of PureGym: it is a comparatively early stage, high-growth enterprise, bringing value by doing differently; extending a core competence through leadership with a vision and an appropriate strategy to achieve it; imitative for sure but with the learning and flexibility that demonstrates that all-important ambidexterity. Nevertheless, we also see that this real-life example does not fit exactly to a normative theoretical construct. Bearing this in mind, our challenge has been to build a framework whereby an organisation can diagnose its entrepreneurial condition and then put together an individual change programme inspired by proven and appropriate practices.

It is assumed that the organisation has, or is in the process of developing, an entrepreneurial vision. In Chapter 3 we saw how such a vision for growth through sustainability and social responsibility was created and shared at Unilever. A generic approach for organisations to create such a vision is the 'minimum viable innovation system' expounded by the consulting firm Innosight in the *Harvard Business Review*.[4]

Regardless of whether the vision is to grow internationally through new technology or to address new consumer trends, the response that we are interested in is the transformation of organisational practices into a sustainable culture based on opportunity recognition and a capacity to change in response to developing circumstances.

Probably the most straightforward way to innovate is to imitate – 'Why aren't we more like them?' but that is more easily said than done – exactly who shall we imitate? As we saw in Chapter 1 (Case 1.2 Neonatal care in the developing world), one size does not fit all. The products, practices and structures of one successful organisation cannot be translated wholesale to another.

Take two British retailers: there is no point trying to impose 'the John Lewis Model' on Marks & Spencer – the first is an employee-owned partnership administered by a trust, the latter is a public limited company responsible to its shareholders. Both do well, but in their own way. The imperatives for retailers are almost identical but the structures are not. The tenth-largest business organisation in Spain, with more than 250 companies, selling into 150 countries and with almost 75,000 employees, is a co-operative: the Mondragon Corporation. Its practices and principles are unlikely to match those of two of the top twenty conglomerates in the US: Koch Industries Inc. or Cargill Inc.; both privately owned. Companies may have ups and downs, they may go bust tomorrow, but all the above examples are highly successful and long established, with an enviable record of innovation. Crucially they are not all the same. Family businesses operate on different time scales to venture capitalists. Non-profit social enterprises have different goals from profit-making ones, although both may be equally concerned with long-term sustainability. And as we saw when considering leadership and alignment there is an interplay of multiple motivations within the culture of any enterprise.

And so we have to move beyond simple imitation: the entrepreneurial mindset, the behaviour, that we are trying to encourage, is all about recognising opportunities, coming up with alternatives and choosing the best one. There are no 'right' answers, but don't forget there are plenty of wrong ones! We can deconstruct the operations of successful organisations to inspire options that might be appropriate for our organisation. The diagnostic tool that we have been working towards does just that.

9.3 A diagnostic framework for entrepreneurial practices

The following framework seeks to diagnose the entrepreneurial practices of an organisation and suggest appropriate actions to make the whole organisation more entrepreneurial in character.

How it works:

Recall the case study (1.2) from Chapter 1. We saw how a simple grid could inspire a range of alternatives from which the most effective could be selected. The grid shown in Table 9.1 develops that principle for an organisational setting.

Column one: diagnosing current practices

Provide answers to the questions from each row in turn in column one to reveal the existing provision of key elements of entrepreneurial practice as highlighted in each chapter of the text. It is recommended that practices deployed over the previous five years be captured here so that the relationship between practices and innovative outcomes can be established. The expectation is that a number of areas will be highlighted where current practices are not capable of delivering the desired future innovative outcomes.

Columns two, three and four: opportunities

Where there are shortfalls between current practices and desired innovative outcomes, then potential new approaches can be explored using columns two, three and four. Examples from throughout the text from other organisations facing analogous shortfalls may be used. As a first step, populate the boxes in the next three columns with a short description of a possible response. Not all need be filled; some will contain several options.

Column five: decisions

For each question in the first column, go back across the row and compare the options. The comparison criteria will vary from one organisation to another – suitability, practicality, effectiveness and so on – but will reflect return on investment. Is it worth doing?

Choose the most appropriate course of action and delegate responsibilities by detailing what needs to be done, by whom and when. The responses in this column are constituents of a change management strategy.

Following this approach, we commonly see somewhat overwhelmed managers diagnosing what is wrong and prescribing wholesale change in response to the conclusion that existing capabilities are unable to deliver the desired level of innovation. Research into change management, however, cautions against attempting to change structures, processes, systems and rules simultaneously. In her seminal work on changing complex systems, Donella Meadows advocates a priority order for change that can provide a useful guide for managers faced with a sequencing dilemma.[5] She suggests that the most effective start point is changing the practices that set the values and goals of the organization. From our diagnostic this would be the practices that the organization uses to create innovation challenges and the practices to recruit and reward individuals for entrepreneurship. By prioritising changes in these areas, managers would then be able to go on to change structures, processes and information systems as necessary.

In reality, we often observe managers prioritising the seemingly 'easier' changes in practices such as changes in information systems and organisational structure. Yet such changes prove difficult to deploy as significant resistance is provoked amongst a workforce with legacy values and goals that are seemingly incompatible with the proposed changes.

In sum, Table 9.1 is provided as a guide for the practices that are most likely to need changing if the organisations capabilities are not delivering the requisite innovation outcomes. To achieve such change requires, somewhat counter-intuitively, managers to first address those areas that they instinctively believe are the most resistant to change.

9.4 Examples of entrepreneurial change programmes

The diagnostic questions have been suggested within each of the previous chapters – and answers *may* be found based on examples found within the text. But remember, it is not the case that 'one-size-fits-all'. To continue this metaphor from the garment trade, there are 'off-the-rack' answers to be had, which

120 Building an Entrepreneurial Organisation

Table 9.1 Diagnostic framework for entrepreneurial practices

	Diagnosis of current practices (1)	What can we do better? (2)	What can we do without? (3)	What can we do differently? (4)	Actions: who, what, when (5)
Can existing capabilities deliver appropriate types of innovation?					
How is the organisation structured for entrepreneurship?					
How are people recruited and rewarded for entrepreneurship?					
What organisational processes support or constrain entrepreneurship?					
How are innovation-challenges identified?					
How is entrepreneurship practised with external stakeholders?					
How does the organisation manage uncertainty and failure?					
How does the organisation reconcile exploratory and exploitative learning?					

could be 'tailored to fit'; better answers may be 'made-to-measure' and the best will be 'bespoke'.

Below we address each diagnostic question in turn and provide examples of how organisations have addressed shortfalls in each specific area of practice. The examples are all drawn from outside this text to reinforce the 'no correct answer' message of the whole book. The 'answers' given here range from simple techniques to the establishment of international standards; the organisations from a family business to a tech giant; the sectors include retail, entertainment and public policy. For any organisation facing analogous shortfalls in practices these examples may provide a helpful start point when considering potential alternative approaches.

1 **Can existing capabilities deliver appropriate types of innovation?**

Example: A traditional circus.

Diagnosis of current practices: A traditional circus has capabilities in managing exotic animals and 'superstar' performers. These have been incrementally improved over time but cannot be easily extended to address consumer concerns voiced on social media platforms about animal rights and the ubiquity of acrobatic performances provided via social media platforms.

Enhancements of current practices – doing better: A small number of traditional circuses have survived but operate in a red ocean[6] with very low margins and little differentiation.

Simplifications of current practices – doing without: A re-invention of a genre that was seen as moribund has been achieved through stripping away what many would have thought key elements (ringmaster, animals, star performers) to leave the capability of acrobatics and clowning, juggling, fire eating and the like provided by lower cost 'unknown' performers. The best known case in point is Cirque du Soleil which has created a blue ocean all of its own.[7]

Alternatives to current practices – doing differently: Cirque du Soleil has expanded internationally through extending its capabilities to offer theatrical themes to its performances, thereby enabling additional revenue streams such as DVD sales, merchandising and premium customer pricing.

2 **How is the organisation structured for entrepreneurship?**

Example: Rolls-Royce Aerospace.

Diagnosis of current practices: In the 1970s, Rolls-Royce Aerospace was structured to focus upon the deployment of fundamental research within their new products. This structure championed the adoption of a radical new carbon fibre turbine blade within their next generation products. However, this technology failed unexpectedly under testing and the organisation was nearly bankrupted by the massive over-investment in what proved to be a too-early-stage technology.

Simplifications of current practices – doing without: Following this experience, the organisation significantly reduced its radical innovation efforts and benchmarked its innovation structure against entrepreneurial organisations in different industries, such as 3M, Whirlpool and Procter & Gamble.

Alternatives to current practices – doing it differently: Over the next 40 years, Rolls-Royce built a structure for innovation that has become a synonym for the gold-plated approach. Its structure is configured around three innovation horizons: 5, 10 and 20 years; seamlessly addressing incremental and radical innovation challenges they utilise a budget for R&D of £1.2 billion (5.8% of underlying revenue) resulting in more than 600 patents filed in 2014.[8]

3 **How are people recruited and rewarded for entrepreneurship?**

Example: Timpson, the UK high street retailer.

Diagnosis of current practices: Timpson started out as a single-family-owned shop and, despite the decline of foot traffic in the high street, aimed to grow to address the opportunity for services that are difficult to provide online. Their services include shoe repairs, house signs and locksmiths services, car keys, photo processing, dry cleaning, key cutting, locker repairs, engraving jewellery and watch repairs.

Simplifications of current practices – doing without: Despite the perceived wisdom prescribing that a firm can only scale up through the addition of formal recruitment and performance appraisal systems, Timpson simply continued with their simple yet idiosyncratic approach of no formal performance appraisals. Moreover, the company even claims not to have a head office! Around 50 per cent of new recruits are 'friends and family' introduced by colleagues and 10 per cent are ex-prisoners. Most new ideas are generated internally by staff with a high degree of autonomy. The philosophy '*If you treat people well, it is blindingly obvious that they will do a good job*' results in Timpson being regularly mentioned in lists of the best companies to work for. This approach has allowed Timpson to expand to 1,475 branches and record revenues of almost £170m.[9] John Timpson himself still visits every single shop once each year.

4   **What organisational processes support or constrain entrepreneurship?**

Example: Military Air Campaign Planners.

Diagnosis of current practices: As part of the development process, an algorithm to significantly enhance battlefield response to air attacks was reviewed at the final stage before deployment in the field. It became apparent that the algorithm, developed on a super computer, would not be fit for purpose in the field as it would not function effectively on a laptop. The developer making this point was aware of the limitation from the onset of the development, yet, despite there being a strict development protocol, this was the first formal opportunity where they could raise the issue.

Alternatives to the current practices – doing it differently: One simple technique to articulate such potential stumbling blocks at an earlier stage is Gary Klein's idea of the Project Pre-mortem – like a post mortem but *before* the patient dies. The team is asked to imagine a future in which the project has failed and then list reasons why that might have been. Asking what *did* happen is subtly different to asking what *might* happen and achieves a more meaningful critique.[10] Within the air-campaign case the algorithm developers had already created a shortcut that didn't require such great computation power through informally subverting the strict development process. Their shortcut was substituted, and the project went on to be highly successful.

5   **How are innovation challenges identified?**

Example: Unilever – low fat ice cream

Diagnosis of current practices: Ice cream sales at Unilever were under threat due to copycat products from rivals in conjunction with consumer demands for healthier products. Unilever had to develop innovation challenges that would meet the entrepreneurial vision of sales growth whilst reducing environmental impact and enhancing social responsibility.[11]

Enhancements of current practices – doing better: The research and consumer insight teams identified the challenge of making ice cream healthier in a protectable way as a method to reach their vision. The technical team identified a novel, patentable protein that could be added to ice cream and would allow for a reduction in the amount of fat and also an increase in the fruit content without compromising texture.

Simplifications of current practices – doing without: As the technology was shared with the development team, team members identified the challenge of how to scale up the production of the protein. Unilever did not have the capability to manufacture this particular ingredient and so, unusually for them, they decided to create the new ingredient with another organisation that did have a proven capability in this area, and could do so in an environmentally efficient way.

Alternatives to current practices – doing it differently: The safety team at Unilever identified the challenge of gaining safety, regulatory and consumer approval for the new protein. The team worked closely with regulatory and safety authorities worldwide to demonstrate the safety and health benefits of the protein. The team also worked with environmental organisations such as Greenpeace to highlight the positive environmental impact of the ingredient when compared to many traditional food products. As a result, many low-fat products and novelty 'popsicle' products were approved for sale in the US, Mexico, China, Philippines and Australia.

6 **How is entrepreneurship practised with external stakeholders?**

Example: Greggs – UK retail bakers.

Diagnosis of current practices: In 2014 the retail bakery chain Greggs launched a loyalty app for mobile phones which gives customers new ways of ordering and paying for products, along with special offers, whilst also (as with all loyalty cards and schemes) allowing the company to monitor sales and behaviours.

Alternatives to current practices – doing it differently. Greggs was keen to distance the scheme from its long established presence on social media. 'When it comes to social media, we focus all of our attention on customer engagement – not sales. Content planning is an important part of what we do, and having the capacity to respond quickly to timely events is also important. We plan our content around a calendar, but the team aim to be as responsive as possible and consider what is going on in the wider social scene, keeping us front of mind for our customers.'[12] For instance, Greggs won numerous awards for a campaign in which new doughnuts were promoted as different characters, with social lives and personalities, and customers were encouraged to comment and vote on their favourites. This campaign was the first that Greggs commissioned from an entrepreneurial supplier; over the five-week campaign, it resulted in 1.5 million doughnut sales and 13 million impressions across Facebook and Google search.[13]

7 **How does the organisation manage uncertainty and failure?**

Example: Not just one business but a whole sector – the aircraft industry.

Diagnosis of current practices: It is a fact of life that every major air crash is international news. This has led the airline industry to develop best practice procedures for dealing with uncertainty and failure that other organisations could learn a great deal by emulating.

Enhancements of current practices – doing better. Strange as it might seem, it is no exaggeration to say that every plane crash makes the next flight safer: an investigation is carried out, lessons are learned and procedures changed. We can compare this with many organisations where mistakes are covered up, ignored and forgotten – the only lesson being learned being to cover your back.[14]

8 **How does the organisation reconcile exploratory and exploitative learning?**

Example – Google.

Diagnosis of current practices: We mentioned at the outset that it was too early to judge the long-term entrepreneurial capability of some of the tech giants. In the case of Google, it would seem that some investors have become concerned about high-risk projects like driverless cars and wearable technology. It's a problem of alignment. For some investors, the search engine which was once 'cutting edge' and 'blue sky' has become 'normal' business.

Simplifications of current practices – doing without: Google's answer has been to restructure under a new holding company called 'Alphabet'. High-profile explorative projects have been moved into an independent entity; the exploitative work remains within Google, where continuous improvements of 'business as usual' services such as search and adwords continue. The investors seem to have been appeased, as it is now clearer to them where the money is being spent.[15] However, our thesis regarding the learning benefits of developing ambidextrous individuals across the whole organisation would suggest that the longer-term prospects of those shareholders may now have been significantly eroded.

9.5 Afterword: more than a century of entrepreneurial change at 3M

To close, by way of an afterword, we shall use what we have learned to illustrate and interpret the behaviour of an organisation that has become a byword for innovation, the 3M Company.

By almost any measure we care to make – size, turnover, product range, number of patents – the 3M Company is a force to be reckoned with. In 2016 it had almost 90,000 employees worldwide, operations in about 70 countries, sales in approximately 200 countries and generated revenue of more than $30 billion.[16] It is regularly voted in the top-three innovative companies in the world, along with Apple and Google. The latter, we contend – along with Amazon, Microsoft, Facebook and others – are too young to judge, many still being under the direct influence of their founding entrepreneurs whose charismatic style may be impossible to match. They are yet to pass the baton to the next generation of leadership. Furthermore, they are so fabulously wealthy that returns on investment in research and development have yet to become clear. The 3M Company, on the other hand, has the longevity to make a more instructive study of serial innovation.

One of the first things you notice when reading 3M's own accounts of its history is the way that it addresses our seventh diagnostic question above of how to manage uncertainty and failure. The foundation myth of the company sets a tone of painstaking perseverance:

9.5.1 How does the organisation manage uncertainty and failure?

The Minnesota Mining and Manufacturing Company was founded in 1902 and immediately ran into trouble. The 'corundum' they were mining turned out to be low grade, not fit for purpose as an abrasive. They had, in their own words, 'a worthless mineral, virtually no sales, poor product quality and formidable competition'. It was twelve years before they made any money at all, fourteen before they paid a dividend. The first profitable product was Three-M-ite™, an abrasive cloth. By 1921 they had developed Wetordry™, as the name suggests, a waterproof abrasive paper; it was this product that gave them entry to the burgeoning automotive industry, preparing car bodies for painting. The next big product, Scotch Tape™, was related – masking tape to help achieve the two-toned finish that was fashionable in cars of the 1920s. So the question for us is how did they go from two or three viable products to 55,000 including some of the most iconic brands of the last hundred years.

The 3M story contains much that has become legendary: the idea that R&D staff were able to work on their own projects for 15 per cent of the time, and the reputation for serendipity: Scotchgard™ was discovered by accident and Post-it™ notes were the result of a eureka moment during a church service. But behind the storytelling lies something other than good luck and the company has been very aware of the necessity of building a tradition of innovation.

3M's own account, *A Century of Innovation*,[17] dispels some of the myths and is quite candid about the internal struggles of some innovations.

By comparing 3M's entrepreneurial changes against the remaining seven questions from our diagnostic grid paints a rich picture of exactly *how* the company did it:

9.5.2 Can existing capabilities deliver appropriate types of innovation?

For all their reputation for freethinking, company leaders at 3M rarely take a leap into the complete darkness. In fact, it can be argued that all their products can be tracked, step by step, technology by technology, market by market, back to their first successes.

Although their product range is enormous there are definite links in the chains of R&D: abrasives – wet and dry paper – masking tape. These are all technologies related to surfaces. Sandpaper consists of three elements: the surface material (in this case the abrasive), the substrate (the paper or cloth) and the glue that keeps them together. Sticky tape is even simpler, just the substrate and the adhesive. The greatest accomplishments of the 3M Company are all to do with one or more of these elements. Although, like Nintendo and DeLaRue, there appears to be an enormous distance of travel for the company, in fact there are no great jumps into the unknown. Technologies are developed to support existing products, enhancing and extending the core competencies of the company, allowing expansion into new areas.

Research into substrates led to an expertise in non-woven technology, one result being Scotch-Brite™ cleaning pads, another being Micropore™ surgical tape.

Proficiency in manufacturing sticky tape gives an obvious advantage when it comes to developing audio tape, which leads to magnetic data storage and floppy discs.

An open-minded approach to adhesives leads on the one hand to the Post-it™ note, which does not stick very well, and on the other to the clothes protector Scotchgard™, which in one vital respect does not stick at all!

What is attached to the substrate can be a lot more varied than abrasives. Reflective materials lead in one direction to road signs, in another (eventually) to plasma screen technology.

As has happened from the beginning some of these products break into new markets with new opportunities. Abrasives broke into automotive; sticky tape broke into office supplies; surgical tape into medical supplies; ScotchBrite™ into household and cleaning; reflective materials into safety gear.

9.5.3 How is the organisation structured for entrepreneurship?

The 3M Company's emphasis on research came out of early failure and was driven by the need for quality assurance. Similarly reactive was the stress on patent protection. Building and defending a successful product range was central to the company's early years. CEO William McKnight expressed the spirit in a manual of 1925: 'The time to get closest control of your product is during your manufacturing process. What you do after this is just history, except in isolated cases.' And so from the start, the central innovation hub – the Product Fabrication Laboratory (ProFabLab) – was closely linked to the practicalities of manufacture and sales. Research considering the communication patterns of the firms reinforced this unusual linkage and was still prevalent in

1998 (see *A Century of Innovation: The 3M Story*). Most large organisations have their strongest communication patterns among operations, management and sales. The topic of concern is typified as management urging operations to deliver more from less, such as: 'sales have committed us to deliver more product than you can make … so speed things up'.

By contrast, in 3M the strongest communication was found to be among R&D, marketing and senior management, where the topic of discussion was very different. Here the discourse would be around 'how best can we deploy new technologies to address emerging market needs?'.

9.5.4 How are people recruited and rewarded for entrepreneurship?

It soon became clear to the company that what they called 'a tolerance for tinkerers' was highly effective in attracting and retaining highly individual talents for whom financial gain was not the most important factor. A conducive working environment and culture was valued by the corporate 'misfits'—the people who, by their own admission, didn't seem to fit anywhere else in 3M. The original twenty or so researchers in the ProFabLab were meticulous regarding their working hours. The spare time they all found to pursue individual projects became known as the 15 Per Cent Rule – but it was never a rule, it was permission. Scotchgard™ *was* discovered by accident, but the accident happened in a research lab to scientists who were able to recognise an opportunity and had permission to act on it. It might have been a happy accident but it was an accident waiting to happen, to the right people in the right place; that can hardly be called serendipity. The discoverer, Patsy O'Connell Sherman, had this advice:

> Keep your eyes and mind open, and don't ignore something that doesn't come out the way you expect it to. Just keep looking at the world with inventor's eyes![18]

Recognition doesn't come with huge bonuses but there are peer-reviewed public awards in every department. A career can be pursued without moving (as is traditional in many firms) from technical to management; there are dual promotion paths with matching salary and perks. For instance, one the most highly paid senior managers in the organisation is a world-leading expert in coatings science and yet has no line management responsibility.

9.5.5 What organisational processes support or constrain entrepreneurship?

Once new products are launched, it is business as usual. 3M promulgates powerful brands and trademarks (as the attentive reader will have noticed), strict patent protection and the ruthlessness and pragmatism one would expect from any major corporation. For example: Tartan Track™, an artificial sports surface, was developed in response to an outside request. As the relevant patents

128 *Building an Entrepreneurial Organisation*

began to expire 3M withdrew its interest not only because of competition from Astroturf but also because it wasn't disposable – there was no replacement business.

A marked feature is the coolly objective exiting from past successes such as photocopying and magnetic recording, even though the company may have invented large parts of the technology; the ability to separate business objectives from nostalgia.

Other technologies have been licenced (plasma screens) or spun off (data storage).

Even in a company with the enviable reputation of 3M there is a perpetual struggle to balance the uncertainty of upstream innovation with the very real, tried, tested and profitable downstream procedures of business as usual, even when their own business is innovation: an open-desk culture takes a lot more effort than an open-desk policy. Values take longer to change than written procedures. For example: To re-create the informality of the ProFabLab in the larger context of the company 3M organised a Technical Forum. But it was not easy; of the 400 technical people invited, only 17 attended the inaugural meeting. It takes time to develop a genuine open-desk culture where networking is everyone's responsibility and if someone calls you, you are expected to help.

9.5.6 How are innovation challenges identified?

In 1996, Senior Vice-President (R&D) William Coyne identified six core elements from the early days[19]:

1   Vision.
2   Foresight.
3   Stretch Goals.
4   Empowerment.
5   Communication.
6   Recognition.

The first three are to an extent 'top down' targets, set by senior managers, related to leadership; the second three are about culture. The vision, informed by foresight, sets the stretch goals as the prime driver of innovation. Innovation challenges are expected to deliver 30 per cent of sales from products introduced in the previous four years (set in the 1950s). This was subsequently increased to 35 per cent in the 1990s.

The first three are theory; the second three are practice – engendering the culture that will provide the new ideas, the exploration that has to come before exploitation. 3M specifies to employees how innovation challenges should be identified through addressing customers' articulated and unarticulated needs. Performance against these challenges is then measured through surveying customers to ensure that 3M is pre-eminent not only in identifying but also addressing those challenges.

9.5.7 How is entrepreneurship practised with external stakeholders?

The ideal product for 3M is one that is easy for the customer to use but difficult for competitors to copy; and the only way to surpass that ideal is to make your own product obsolete. The foresight necessary for such continuing innovation comes from a long tradition of working closely with current and potential customers to reveal their unmet needs.

For example, when 3M moved into medical products, senior staff would accompany doctors on their rounds to understand the possibilities. This led to collaborations and partnerships, originally gathering feedback on existing products and prototypes and subsequently developing into working relationships with practitioners and patients, sharing knowledge and learning together.

For a company with so many products it had been difficult for some customers to know quite whom to contact. The 3M response is to assign key account personnel which involves some surrender of power from divisions but results in integrated support by working across the lines.

9.5.8 How does the organisation reconcile exploratory and exploitative learning?

It is the learning across divisions that has proven so effective for 3M. A new discovery is not the end for those involved; they are expected to hawk their pride and joy around the company and try to incorporate it into new product lines. Products belong to divisions but technologies belong to the company – they should be shared. This procedure goes at its own pace: it's time to take a closer look at the legend that is the Post-it note.

The concept of a sticky bookmark which could be removed without harm to the book came about in 1973 when church chorister Arthur Fry kept losing his place in a hymnal. That is the core of truth. But: Art Fry worked his whole career in product development for 3M. As part of his job he attended regular seminars where new discoveries from Central Research were presented in the manner of 'here's the solution – what's the problem?' It was at one of these that he heard of an adhesive developed by Spencer Silver.

The real breakthrough was Fry's changing the usage from a bookmark (small potential market) to a note (larger market than they could ever imagine).

The gap between invention of the adhesive (1968) and the possible application was five years: it would be another eight years before the product was actually launched (in 1981) to less than universal acclaim. It would take a concerted marketing strategy to bring final success. So although there might have been a *eureka* moment, it was a moment experienced by a new product developer who had been made privy to his company's latest research with the express purpose of developing new products.

The greatest challenge for an innovative company comes when it develops a product or service that has not been seen before; where to put it? What happens to ideas that are just not 'normal' – that don't find a home in their own categories? 3M has a system of 'Genesis Grants', peer-allocated to provide seed funding for continuing research into projects to which, according to one of 3M's VPs, Chris Holmes: 'no sensible, conventional person in the company would give money'.[20]

But even a company as experienced as 3M can mismanage the balance. The following account is based on several articles in the financial press.[21]

In December 2000 3M share prices jumped nearly 20 per cent at the news of a new CEO, James McNerney, the first outsider to lead the company in its hundred-year history (with hindsight, perhaps significantly). McNerney was determined to bring a little discipline to a company that was perceived to be slack and underperforming. There are proven formulas for incremental improvement; one of the best known is Six Sigma. It consists of a series of process tools to raise efficiency by reducing wastage and eliminating production defects. It seemed to work, profits grew by an average of 22 per cent. But a price was paid by the creative culture.

In a 2013 interview,[22] 3M ambassador Geoff Nicholson reveals what happened:

> The Six Sigma process killed innovation at 3M. Initially what would happen in 3M with Six Sigma people, they would say they need a five-year business plan for [a new idea]. Come on, we don't know yet because we don't know how it works, we don't know how many customers [will take it up], we haven't taken it out to the customer yet.

This is not to criticise process management, but it needs to be understood. Six Sigma is about continuous improvement and is unlikely to deliver anything radical. Benner and Tushman (2003) argue for the ambidextrous approach because an emphasis on incremental innovation establishes an imbalance. The focus is biased towards easily achievable metrics of efficiency and customer satisfaction – existing capabilities are enhanced but the development of new competencies suffers by comparison.[23]

In the same *Wall Street Journal* interview, McNerney's successor George Buckley confirmed this:

> Six Sigma's worked wonderfully in our factories, but we tried it in our labs and it doesn't work. It's obvious why. The creative process, whether it is with me or anybody else, is a discontinuous process. Creativity comes from freedom, not control.

It is what they had always known, as their Senior Vice President for R&D, William Coyne, argues:

> There are always random events – good and bad – that affect an innovation, the mix of randomness and chaos is always part of the pattern. ... In other words, the fuzzy front-end is inherently fuzzy – and should be.

This is echoed by their Vice President of the electronic group, Gary Pint:

> Innovation is generally an untidy process. A majority of new ideas fail, but people shouldn't fear for their jobs when that happens. We estimate that 60 percent of our formal, new product programs never make it.

And the importance of learning from failure is endorsed by their CEO from 1986 to 1991, Lew Lehr:

> When this happens, the important thing is not to punish the people involved.

But it is controlled freedom, organised chaos; there are fairly strict criteria governing innovation at 3M, as espoused by world renowned chemist and inventor, Sunitra Mitra:

> I tell my younger peers that they must meet two criteria: there must be a market need, whether articulated or unarticulated, and there must be a feasible technical pathway for getting there. That's when things come together.[24]

9.6 Conclusion: building an entrepreneurial organisation

In conclusion, we revisit our exemplar case of 3M and reflect upon its current situation. In 2014, well over a century after incorporation, sales were at an all-time high of $32 billion; up by 4.9 per cent from the previous year. How was this performance achieved?

According to current (2016) CEO Inge G. Thulin, the key building blocks for sustained innovative performance are portfolio management, investing in research and development, and business transformation.[25] Interestingly for us, these three reflect different aspects of entrepreneurial behaviour that we identified at the very start of this book: research and development is all about exploring alternative approaches; portfolio management is all about making choices and business transformation is all about doing things differently.

It is the combination and integration of these behaviours that make *this* organisation entrepreneurial.

References

1 Courtney, H., Lovallo, D. & Clarke, C. (2013, November). 'Deciding how to decide: A toolkit for executives making high risk strategic bets', *Harvard Business Review*, 63–70.
2 www.theguardian.com/business/2016/oct/11/pure-gym-abandons-london-stock-exchange-ipo-plan.

3 www.telegraph.co.uk/finance/newsbysector/retailandconsumer/11337645/Pure-Gym-founder-on-how-he-built-Britains-biggest-gym-chain.html.
4 See https://hbr.org/2014/12/innovation-on-the-fly.
5 Meadows, D. H. (2008). *Thinking in Systems: A Primer*. White River Junction, VT: Chelsea Green Publishing.
6 Kim, W. C. & Mauborgne, R. (2005). *Blue Ocean Strategy: How to Create Uncontested Market Space and Make the Competition Irrelevant*. Cambridge, Mass.: Harvard Business School Press.
7 Kirkham, P., Mosey, S. & Binks, M. (2013). *Ingenuity*. Nottingham, UK: University of Nottingham.
8 See 2014 Annual Report http://ar.rolls-royce.com/2014/.
9 John Timpson has written widely about his business practices, most notably *Upside Down Management: A Common Sense Guide to Better Business* (2010), from Wiley.
10 Klein, G. (2007). 'Performing a project premortem', *Harvard Business Review*, 85(9).
11 See www.unilever.co.uk/innovation for more about the company's innovations in ice cream and elsewhere.
12 See www.bakeryinfo.co.uk/news/fullstory.php/aid/12633/Greggs_92_loyalty_app_achieves_initial_success.html.
13 www.retailtimes.co.uk/doughnut-social-media-campaign-scoops-top-awards-for-bakers-greggs/.
14 The issue is explored more fully here: www.washingtonpost.com/posteverything/wp/2014/06/23/we-all-make-mistakes-but-airlines-are-best-at-learning-from-them/.
15 www.theguardian.com/technology/2015/aug/10/google-alphabet-parent-company.
16 http://solutions.3m.com/wps/portal/3M/en_US/3M-Company/Information/AboutUs/WhoWeAre/.
17 *A Century of Innovation: The 3M Story*: http://multimedia.3m.com/mws/media/171240O/3m-coi-book-tif.pdf.
18 Ibid.
19 Jones, T. (2002). *Innovating at the Edge: How Organizations Evolve and Embed Innovation Capability*. Oxford: Butterworth-Heinemann.
20 Gunther, M. (2010). '3M's innovation revival', *Fortune*, pp. 73–76.
21 See www.bloomberg.com/bw/stories/2007-06-10/at-3m-a-struggle-between-efficiency-and-creativity.
22 *Wall Street Journal*, 1 March, 2010.
23 Benner, M. J. & Tushman, M.L. (2003, April). 'Exploitation, exploration, and process management: The productivity dilemma revisited', *The Academy of Management Review*, 28(2): 238–256.
24 All quotations from 3M executives and scientists can be found in *A Century of Innovation: The 3M Story*: http://multimedia.3m.com/mws/media/171240O/3m-coi-book-tif.pdf.
25 See http://investors.3m.com/financials/annual-reports-and-proxy-statements/default.aspx.

Index

Locators in *italics* refer to figures and those in **bold** to tables.

3M Company: benchmarking 61–2; core competencies 126; entrepreneurial change programme 124–31; external stakeholders 129; innovation 70, 128; organisational learning 129–30; organisational structure 126–7; processes 127–8; recruitment 127; rewarding employees 127; uncertainty 125
90 per cent confidence quiz 89–92, **90**, **91**

absorptive capacity *106*, 106–7
acquisition of knowledge 107, 111; *see also* learning
adaptiveness 10, 108
administrative approach, strategy 23–4
agility 13, 38
aircraft industry, uncertainty management 124
Airfix 13
alliances: learning 105–6; Unilever 44–5
Amazon: cost saving 97; extendibility 26
ambidextrous organisations 102; Disney and Pixar case study 110–13; learning 103 9, 110; structure 109; tacit and explicit knowledge 102–3
ambiguity 8
Anytown Wanderers AFC 32–4
Apple 10, 25
automotive industry, blue ocean strategy **29**, 29–31

bank account switching 94
behaviours 11; *see also* culture of entrepreneurship
benchmarking: culture of entrepreneurship 61–2; learning 105–6

Benincasa, Robyn 56–7
best practice innovation process 75
Bigmouthmedia 52
bliss points 24
blue ocean strategy 28–31, 121
Borlaug, Norman 9
Buckley, George 130
A Bug's Life 112
bureaucratic structures 47, 49
business as usual 8, 24, 124, 127–8
business fade, Unilever case study 40–1
business schools' strategy 22

capabilities *see* core competencies
champions of innovation 54–5
change *see* organisational change
change management 119
Chesborough, Henry 76–7
Cirque du Soleil case study 120–1
climate of entrepreneurship 68–9; *see also* culture of entrepreneurship
Coca-Cola, core competencies 26–7
codifying strategy, Unilever 38–9
combination, innovation 75–6
communications technology development 9
competitive advantage, culture of entrepreneurship 49, 51–2; *see also* 'what can we do better?'
competitive differentiation, core competencies 25
complexity 8
computer-generated imagery (CGI) 111
confidence quiz 89–92, **90**, **91**
Connect + Develop 77
construction toys 13, 77
convergent thinking 70

core business 13
core competencies: 3M Company 126; Amazon 26; Apple 25; circus example 120–1; Coca-Cola 26–7; Ford 25; Google 27; Honda 25; knowledge 103; strategy 24–7; Toyota 26; Unilever 41–5
cosmetics market 44–5
cost saving, tailoring case study 97–9
Coughlan, Peter 78–9
Coyne, William 130
creative destruction 7, 10
creativity: and innovation 3–4, 5, 6, 67; people 51–2, 65–6
Crilly, Jim 36; *see also* culture of entrepreneurship in practice (Unilever); strategy in practice (Unilever)
crisis: as driver of innovation 9–10, 12–13; growth model 11–12
crowdsourcing 79–80
culture of entrepreneurship 47, 57; failure 68, 100–1; leadership 54–7; organisational structure 47–9, *48*; people 51–4; processes 50–1; venture-led innovation 94
culture of entrepreneurship in practice (Unilever case study) 59, 70–2; importance of 59–62; leadership 68–70; processes 68–70; recruitment 65–6; rewarding employees 66–8; structure 62–5, 68–70
customer understanding: core competencies 25; uncertainty 94–5

De La Rue PLC 13
decision making: diagnostic framework 119; paradigm innovation 14; project selection case study 81–6; Unilever 45
design 5, 6
development process strategy 39–41, *42*
diagnostic case-based approach, entrepreneurial change programme 115–18
diagnostic framework, entrepreneurial change programme 118–19, **120**
differentiation *see* competitive advantage; 'what can we do differently?'
directive style 66
discovery 4, 6
Disney case study 110–13
disruption: dynamic capabilities 27–8; and innovation 4; open innovation 77
'distance of travel' 13

divergent thinking 66, 69–70, 71
diversity, recruitment 65–6
'doing better' *see* 'what can we do better?'
'doing differently' *see* 'what can we do differently?'
'doing without' *see* 'what can we do without?'
Dyer, J. H. 55
dynamic capabilities 27–8
Dyson, James 56

Ehrlich, Paul 22–3
eliminate-reduce-raise-create (ERRC) actions 30–1, **31**
Elizabeth Arden cosmetics 44–5
embedded learning 103–5
employees *see* human resources management; people
entrepreneurial analysis 8–9
entrepreneurial change programmes 115, 131; 3M Company 124–31; case-based diagnostic approach 115–18; diagnostic framework 118–19, **120**; examples of 119–24
entrepreneurial culture *see* culture of entrepreneurship
entrepreneurial strategy *see* strategy
entrepreneurs as individuals 1–2
entrepreneurship: definition 1–3; and innovation 1–2, 7–9
explicit knowledge 102–3, *104*
exploitative learning 107–10, 124, 129
explorative learning 107, 108–10, 124, 129
extendibility, core competencies 26
external change: drivers 12; strategy 22
external stakeholders 73; 3M Company 129; combining and recombining 75–6; different approaches 78–80; Greggs 123–4; network approach 73–5; opening up 76–7, **78**; project selection case study 81–6
extreme users 78–9
extrinsic motivation 67–8

failure: 3M Company 125; culture of entrepreneurship 68, 100–1; learning from 96; management 100–1; processes 51; tailoring case study 97–9
feedback 74–5, 79, 95, 129; *see also* measuring improvement
Feynman, Richard 101
FIFA 32–4

FMCGs (fast-moving consumer goods): culture of entrepreneurship 65–6; innovation 13; strategy 39
football, innovation case study 32–4
Ford, competitive differentiation 25
Ford, Henry 2–3, 6
fractal planes 39–40
freedom: for employees 66, 68, 69, 71; for managers 52–3
Friedman, Milton 9
Furr, N. R. 55

gatekeepers 54
Google: core competencies 27; innovation 10; organisational learning 105–6, 124
Greggs 123–4
Greiner, Larry 11–12
growth model 11–12
growth of organisations: maintaining innovation 49, 60–1; structure 48–9
Gulati, Ranjay 59–60

Hamel, Gary 24–6
Haragdon, Andrew 75
health care, neonatal care case study 14–19
hierarchy, organisational structure 48–9
high street shops 13–14
historical cases, innovation 74
HMV 13–14
Honda 25
Hoover 56
Howe, J. 79
human resources management: culture of entrepreneurship 48–9, *49*, 51–4; processes 53, 68–70; *see also* leadership; people

ice cream, product development example 43–4, 122–3
imitation 10
improvement 4; *see also* measuring improvement
incentives *see* motivation
incremental innovation 7, 9, 11; ambidextrous organisations 109–10; blue ocean strategy 28–30
incrementalism 23
incubators for neonatal care case study 14–19
individual entrepreneurs 1–2
individuals *see* people
in-house innovation: historical 74; uncertainty 94

innovation: contingency approach 17–19; and creativity 3–4, 5, 6, 67; culture of entrepreneurship 59–60; definitions 5–6; drivers of 9–10, 12; and entrepreneurship 1–2, 7–9; external stakeholders 73–4; forms of 6–7; incremental vs radical 7, 11; processes 70, 74–5; uncertainty classification *92*, 92–3; understanding 3–5
innovation challenges: 3M Company 128; determining 12–17; motivation 62–5; uncertainty 92–3; Unilever 122–3
innovation champions 54–5
internal change: drivers 12; strategy 22
intrinsic motivation 67–8
invention 4, 5, 6
iterative approaches 21, 74

Jobs, Steve 55
jobs for life 8

Kim, W. C. 28, 30
knowledge: organisational capability 106–8; organisational learning 103–5, 110; tacit and explicit 102–3
Kodak 12, 42, 88–9

laissez faire style 66
Lane, P. J. 107
language use, strategy 37
leadership: culture of entrepreneurship 54–7, 68–70; failure 100–1; strategy 37, 39; styles 56–7, 66–7; Unilever 68–70
lean approach: 3M Company 130; strategy 23; uncertainty 94
learning, ambidextrous organisations 103–9, 110
Lego 13, 77
Lehr, Lew 131
lettuce packaging example 59–60
life cycle, organisational 47
'lifetimes' (organisations) 11
loose-tight management 69
Lubatkin, M. 107

Magnum 43–4
mainstream users 78–9
management: absorptive capacity 107; accessibility of 68–9; change 119; core competencies 27–8; entrepreneurial vs administrative 23–4; failure 100–1; freedom 70, 71; styles 66–7; uncertainty 88–92, 94–6, 100–1, 124;

vs leadership 56–7; *see also* culture of entrepreneurship; human resources management
market research: external stakeholders 78; tailoring case study 98; uncertainty 93, 94, 98
marketing: crowdsourcing 79–80; extreme users 78–9; online communities 79–80
Marks & Spencer ready meals 4–5
Mauborgne, R. 28, 30
mavericks 66–7
McNerney, James 130
measuring improvement 11; 3M Company 125, 131; culture of entrepreneurship 50; feedback 74–5, 79, 95, 129; peer review 112–13
Meccano 13
Miele 104
Military Air Campaign Planners 122
Minnesota Mining and Manufacturing Company *see* 3M Company
Mintzberg, Henry 23, 48
mission: meaning of 37; Unilever 38
Mitra, Sinitra 131
mobile phone development 9
motivation: case studies 121–2, 127; innovation challenges 63–5; intrinsic vs extrinsic 67–8; rewarding employees 52–4, 66–8
multinational organisations, strategy 36; *see also individually named companies e.g. Unilever*
My Starbucks Idea 79–80

neonatal care case study 14–19, **18**
Nesta **78**, 78, 82
Netflix: absorptive capacity 107; people 52–3
network approach, external stakeholders 73–5
networking, strategy 45
90 per cent confidence quiz 89–92, **90**, **91**
Nintendo 13
nostalgia 13

online communities 79–80
online retail: Amazon 26, 97; tailoring case study 97–9
open innovation **76**, 76–7, **78**
opportunity recognition 9–10; diagnostic framework 118–19; entrepreneurial change programmes 116–18; strategy 22, 23–4

optioning, strategy 40
organic structures 48–9
organisational change: blue ocean strategy 28–31; change management 119; external stakeholders 76–7; innovation champions 54–5; learning 106–8, 110–11; status quo 54–6; structure 47–9; understanding 10–12; Unilever case study 41–2, 59–62; *see also* entrepreneurial change programmes
organisational learning 103–5, 110; 3M Company 129–30; Disney and Pixar case study 110–13; Google 105–6, 124
organisational life cycle 47
organisational structure: 3M Company 126–7; ambidextrous organisations 109; culture of entrepreneurship 47–9, *48*, 62–5, 68–70; Rolls-Royce 121; Unilever 62–5, 68–70

packaging, lettuce example 60
paradigm innovation 6, 14, 30–1; *see also* radical innovation
participative style 66
peer review 112–13
people: appraisals 53; culture of entrepreneurship 51–4; recruitment 52, 65–6, 121–2, 127; rewarding 52–4, 66–8, 121–2, 127; *see also* leadership
performance *see* measuring improvement
Pint, Gary 131
pioneering *see* radical innovation
Pixar case study 110–13
planning: culture of entrepreneurship 50; strategy 39, 41
population forecasting example 22–3
position innovation 6
Prahalad, C. K. 24–6
predictability 11; uncertainty 88–92; Unilever case study 38
pricing, Unilever case study 40–1
process innovation 6, 11, 18
processes: 3M Company 127–8; culture of entrepreneurship 53, 68–70; innovation 70, 74–5; Military Air Campaign Planners 122; uncertainty and success 96
Procter & Gamble: learning 105–6; open innovation 77; product development 51
product development 43–4, 51
product innovation 6; leadership 55, 56; packaging 60–1; Unilever case study 41
project selection case study 81–6
public sector 13
PureGym case study 116–18

R&D at Unilever: core competencies 41–5; culture of entrepreneurship 61–2; strategy 37
radical innovation 7, 11; ambidextrous organisations 108–10; blue ocean strategy 28–9; *see also* paradigm innovation
ready meals example 4–5
recombinant innovation 75–6, **76**
recruitment 52, 65–6; 3M Company 127; Timpson 121–2
red oceans 29
resilience 13
reviewing: individuals 52–3; strategy 40
rewarding employees 52–4, 66–8; 3M Company 127; Timpson 121–2
Ries, Eric 23
risk 11–12, 112
role planning 49, 52–3
Rolls-Royce 53, 121
Rothwell, R. 74, 74–5

Sagan, Carl 101
sales, as validation 94–5, 99
Salinas Valley example 59–60
scanning: culture of entrepreneurship 50; strategy 40
Schumpeter, Joseph Alois 2, 7, 10
Shnuggle 80
Simon, Julian 22–3
SIMPL (Simplified Initiative Management and Product Launch) 51
Six Sigma 130
skills, core competencies 26–7
social media 63
Sony 12
SpinBrush concept 77
Starbucks 79–80
start-ups: failure 97–100; tailoring case study 97–9; uncertainty 94–6
status quo 54–6
strategy 21; core competencies 24–7; 'doing differently' 28–9, 30–1; dynamic capabilities 27–8; entrepreneurial approaches 22–4; language use 37; paradigm innovation 30–1; red vs blue oceans 28–31; traditional approaches 22
strategy in practice (football case study) 31–4
strategy in practice (Unilever case study) 36, 45–6; alliances 44–5; codifying 38–9; core competencies 41–5; decision making 45; definition of 37–8;
development process 39–41; need for 36–7; product development 43–4
structure *see* organisational structure
success factors: ambidextrous organisations 102, 109, 111–12; codifying strategy 38, 43; culture of entrepreneurship 47, 48, 50, 54, 57, 70–1; entrepreneurial change programmes 117–18, 126; and innovation 3, 10–11; recruitment 65; rewarding employees 66; uncertainty management 88, 94–6; *see also* measuring improvement
SWOT analysis (Strengths, Weaknesses, Opportunities and Threats) 22

tacit knowledge 102–3, *104*
tailoring case study 97–9
technology: computer-generated imagery (CGI) 111; strategy development process 41–2, 43–4
Tesla Roadster 29–30, **31**
Threadless 80
Timpson 121–2
Total Quality Management (TQM) 61–2
Toy Story 111–12
Toyota: core competencies 26; knowledge 103, *104*, 106
traditional approaches, strategy 22
traditional innovation *see* in-house innovation
training, culture of entrepreneurship 66
transformation, learning 107

uncertainty 8; 3M Company 125; aircraft industry 124; decision-making approaches 14; innovation challenges classification 92, 92–3; management 88–92, 94–6, 100–1; tailoring case study 97–9; use of processes 50–1
Unilever: FMCGs (fast-moving consumer goods) 13; innovation challenges 122–3; job for life case study 8; R&D 37, 41–5, 61–2; *see also* culture of entrepreneurship in practice (Unilever); strategy in practice (Unilever)

validation 93–4, 99
value for customers: core competencies 25; uncertainty 94–5
value through innovation 8, 75–6
values, meaning of 37
venture-led innovation 94

vision 37, 38; meaning of 37
volatility 8
VUCA (volatility, uncertainty, complexity and ambiguity) 8

W. L. Gore & Associates 73–4
'what can we do better?' 7; aircraft industry 124; Cirque du Soleil 121; Disney 111; neonatal care case study **18**, 18; Unilever ice cream 123

'what can we do differently?': automotive industry 28–31; Cirque du Soleil 121; Disney 111; innovation 7, 8; neonatal care case study **18**; PureGym 117; Unilever ice cream 123

'what can we do without?': automotive industry 30–1; Cirque du Soleil 121; Google 124; neonatal care case study **18**, 18; Rolls-Royce 121; Timpson 122; Unilever ice cream 123